Building Effective Learning Environments

Teachers are bombarded with trends and competing ideas. This book provides a framework to help you find the right balance between new and old instructional practices, so you can design learning environments that truly enhance learning.

The author shares key research-based principles to engage and extend learning, and he debunks common myths. He then shows how to use a classical method and how to engage with new ideas and evidence to create a highly effective learning environment. Each chapter offers reflection and application questions you can use independently or in book studies to get the most out of your reading.

Written for teachers of any grade level, the book contains applications and examples across content areas so you can see how to implement the ideas in your own classroom or school.

Kevin S. Krahenbuhl, Ed.D. is Associate Professor of Education and Program Director for the *Assessment, Learning, and Student Success Ed.D. Program* at Middle Tennessee State University. He has spent his entire professional life in public schools and is committed to working with public schools to improve learning for all students. He is also author of *The Decay of Truth in Education* (Cambridge Scholars Publishing, 2018).

Also Available from Eye On Education
www.routledge.com/k-12

The Elements of Education for Teachers:
50 Research-Based Principles Every Educator Should Know
Austin Volz, Julia Hidgon, William Lidwell

Rigor Is Not a Four-Letter Word, 3e
Barbara R. Blackburn

Working Hard, Working Happy:
Cultivating a Culture of Effort and Joy in the Classroom
Rita Platt

Moving from What to What If?
Teaching Critical Thinking with Authentic Inquiry and Assessments
John Barell

Teaching Students to Dig Deeper, 2e:
10 Essential Skills for College and Career Readiness
Ben Johnson

Authentic Assessment in Social Studies:
A Guide to Keeping It Real
David Sherrin

Building Effective Learning Environments

A Framework for Merging the Best of Old and New Practices

Kevin S. Krahenbuhl

Taylor & Francis Group

NEW YORK AND LONDON

First published 2021
by Routledge
605 Third Avenue, New York, NY 10017

and by Routledge
2 Park Square, Milton Park, Abingdon, Oxon, OX14 4RN

Routledge is an imprint of the Taylor & Francis Group, an informa business

© 2021 Kevin S. Krahenbuhl

The right of Kevin S. Krahenbuhl to be identified as author of this work has been asserted by him in accordance with sections 77 and 78 of the Copyright, Designs and Patents Act 1988.

All rights reserved. No part of this book may be reprinted or reproduced or utilised in any form or by any electronic, mechanical, or other means, now known or hereafter invented, including photocopying and recording, or in any information storage or retrieval system, without permission in writing from the publishers.

Trademark notice: Product or corporate names may be trademarks or registered trademarks, and are used only for identification and explanation without intent to infringe.

Library of Congress Cataloging-in-Publication Data
Names: Krahenbuhl, Kevin S., author.
Title: Building effective learning environments: a framework for merging the best of old and new practices/Kevin S. Krahenbuhl.
Description: New York, NY: Routledge, 2021. | Includes bibliographical references.
Identifiers: LCCN 2020052985 (print) | LCCN 2020052986 (ebook) | ISBN 9780367743581 (hardback) | ISBN 9780367720865 (paperback) | ISBN 9781003157441 (ebook)
Subjects: LCSH: Instructional systems–Design. | Effective teaching. | Classroom environment.
Classification: LCC LB1028.38 .K73 2021 (print) | LCC LB1028.38 (ebook) | DDC 371.3–dc23
LC record available at https://lccn.loc.gov/2020052985
LC ebook record available at https://lccn.loc.gov/2020052986

ISBN: 978-0-367-74358-1 (hbk)
ISBN: 978-0-367-72086-5 (pbk)
ISBN: 978-1-003-15744-1 (ebk)

Typeset in Palatino
by KnowledgeWorks Global Ltd.

Dedication

I dedicate this book to my family. To my wife, Allison, whom I have the great blessing of being married to over all these years. This work is in great part inspired by your love for teaching our children and my desire to link what I do to the tremendous work you do for our children. I am so thankful for your commitment to our children, to our home, and to our marriage and this work is in some ways just another of my lifelong efforts to court you.

To my children, who are the greatest gifts I could have ever imagined, I dedicate this book to you and your future. I have written this work in hope that it will make a meaningful difference in the lives of others whom you will one day run this world with. Your generation will, I hope, be able to stop the trend of our country towards disharmony and reemphasize the universal things that we all hold in common as children of God. As I dedicate this to you, I will close with the words of the Apostle Paul to the Church at Ephesus:

> [4]Rejoice in the Lord always. I will say it again: Rejoice![5] Let your gentleness be evident to all. The Lord is near.[6] Do not be anxious about anything, but in every situation, by prayer and petition, with thanksgiving, present your requests to God.[7] And the peace of God, which transcends all understanding, will guard your hearts and your minds in Christ Jesus.
>
> [8]Finally, brothers and sisters, whatever is true, whatever is noble, whatever is right, whatever is pure, whatever is lovely, whatever is admirable – if anything is excellent or praiseworthy – think about such things.[9] Whatever you have learned or received or heard from me, or seen in me – put it into practice. And the God of peace will be with you.
>
> **Ephesians 4:4–9,** *New International Version Translation*

Contents

Acknowledgements   viii
Meet the Author   x
Introduction   xi

Part I
Foundations: What Do We Need to Know?

1   Principles to Engage Learning   3

2   Principles to Extend Learning   20

3   Learning Myths and Other Nonsense   34

Part II
Framework: How Do We Do This?

4   The Trivium: A Classical Method   51

5   Engaging with New Ideas and Evidence   65

6   The 21st Century Trivium Framework   85

7   Instructional Principles   103

8   Application in Specific Content Areas   129

9   Conclusion   149

Appendix A: The Dime   153
Appendix B: Dr. K's Checklist for Evaluating Scientific Claims on Learning   154
Appendix C: Dr. K's What's in the Ballpark Activity (Blank Copy)   156
References   157

Acknowledgements

This work is a fusion of ideas derived from many other works that inspired me as well as my own unique signature. As such, I wish to first thank all those who have engaged in objective science of learning and their dissemination of the findings. This work is a product informed and built upon the work of others and so while I cannot list every contributor individually, this opening acknowledgement is made with you in mind.

In addition to the necessity to offer acknowledgement to those whom I have learned so much from and from whom I will continue to engage, I also wish to offer thanks to those who challenged my thinking. Included among these are scholars who, in many ways, operate from a completely different worldview, as well as colleagues and students who sharpen my thinking through the crucible of application and discourse. The discussions about learning, about teaching, about creativity, about assessment, about school improvement, and so on, with persons holding varied views has refined many of the ways I think about things. Steel sharpens steel and I am thankful for those with whom I disagree and all those whose challenges have helped refine my understanding and make my claims and understanding more precise.

I also wish to acknowledge the team from Routledge/Taylor & Francis. In particular, Lauren Davis, whose interest in the proposal initiated a fruitful relationship that has improved the initial work. The peer reviewers offered helpful critiques to improve the precision and focus of this work, Mrs. Davis whose continued review and feedback did likewise, and to the other staff involved who help bring this idea to reality. I am honored to have Routledge/Taylor & Francis publish this work.

Finally, I must acknowledge my family for its support in all that I do. First and foremost, to God Almighty for whom I am so grateful for the opportunity to live in this time when I am not completely swept away by cultural prosperity but challenged, which helps keep my focus on things that matter more than just the ephemeral feelings and wealth most of us are consumed by. Second, to my parents, my brother, and sisters whom I am so blessed to call family. Each of you has influenced me to an extent you cannot fully understand and I am so thankful for the love that each of you has offered to me even when we do not always see eye to eye. And last, but not least, I must acknowledge my wife and children. My passion for observing the world, reading about things of interest, and studying them scientifically often keeps me busy but you stand by me, graciously welcoming me home after a long day and waving to me as I leave each day. My Father in Heaven and my family are my great rocks in life and I wish to acknowledge them as such for without that firm foundation I would not be able to accomplish this work nor anything else. I must acknowledge your crucial role in helping me complete the work I am so honored to do.

It is my great hope that in the near future we can see education emerge as a leading industry for evidence-informed practice and simultaneously the training of students who revere that objective pursuit of general truths with respect for nuance but the wisdom to discern between the two. I hope that this work is a meaningful contribution towards that end.

Meet the Author

Kevin S. Krahenbuhl, Ed.D. is Program Director for the *Assessment, Learning, and Student Success Ed.D. Program* at Middle Tennessee State University that includes concentrations in both K12 school improvement and higher education. He has spent his entire professional life in public schools and is committed to working with public schools to improve learning for all students. Additionally, he and his wife homeschool their children using the principles laid out in this manual and readily acknowledges that we both need public education and need to carefully consider what is best in light of the context of each unique circumstance. Dr. Krahenbuhl has published dozens of peer reviewed articles, book chapters, popular level articles, and conference presentations. His first book, published in February 2018 is entitled, *The Decay of Truth in Education* where he provided a defense for the importance that educators hold for truth when it comes to learning. He lives in Murfreesboro, Tennessee, with his wife, Allison, and their four children: Audrey, Ethan, Sophie, and Ava.

Introduction

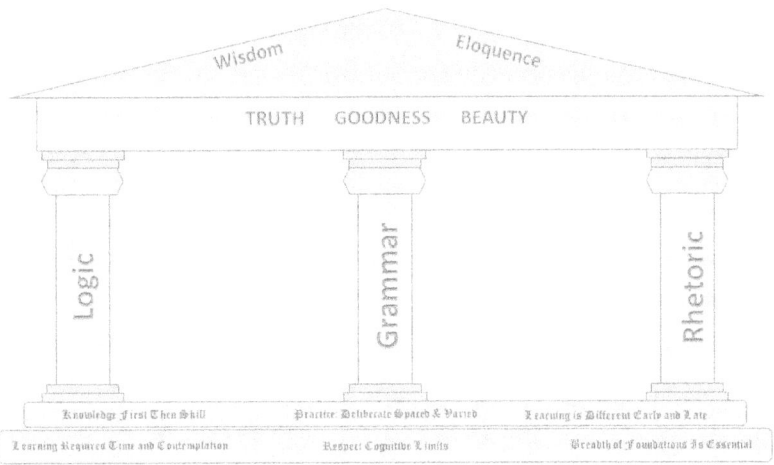

The educational system of a society serves in many ways as a kind of reflective pool. When one looks at the educational system of a society, they see reflections of (a) what is, and if they peer deeper into the pool, they can get a glimpse of (b) what is to come. Education in the present has particular aims and through those, you can see *what is the state of affairs* for that society through considering what is prioritized. Looking a little bit more deeply, education also gives us a lens with which to see into the future of *what is to come*. For any society in which the majority of its populace are educated through schools, the dominant philosophy of the schoolroom in one generation is likely to be the dominant philosophy of governance in the next.

Given this two-way reflective nature of education and the myriad of calls for educational change, for reform, for a return, and even for a complete overhaul, it is worthy of reflecting on what type of educational system our society has – and what we can do about it (individually and collectively). Because of the monumental influence that education has on future generations, education has received considerable attention from disparate groups. On one end of the spectrum, there are visionaries who imagine something radically different. These visionaries tend to pose questions like: How could schools look different? What will the future look like? What is possible for schooling? On the other end, there are traditionalists who yearn to conserve the best of a society as the basis for ensuring its success moving forward. These traditionalists tend to pose different questions such as: What are the most important aspects of education to preserve? What can we learn from the past to inform our path into the future? Somewhere in the middle of these ends of the spectrum fall others who we might simply call pragmatists – those who are interested primarily in the here and now or simply prioritizing the benefit for the individual. The pragmatists would pose different questions: What has immediate relevance to learners' personal and professional lives? How can schools improve preparation for successful careers? What is the best way to make schooling personally relevant? These varied voices have led to divergent approaches to reform being proposed and arguably is a factor in the pattern of teachers to see each new educational change in light of the phrase: *This too shall pass*. But reforming and improving education is something we are all committed to – visionaries, traditionalists, and pragmatists – albeit we have different purposes and aims.

It is in this way that I hope to offer this book as a resource for us to imagine the possibilities of something likely to make a meaningful difference in improving student learning independent of where you fall on that spectrum. I am not advocating a one-size-fits-all approach for teaching but rather a framework that is tested through the ages while also being supported by the latest and greatest in research on learning. This framework is malleable and scalable and can be meaningfully integrated into what you are doing with your students to help equip them with tools for learning. And so, while it does not offer a one-size-fits-all panacea, it does offer a systematic approach to improving the structure and design of your curriculum, your assessments, your instruction, and consequently, your students' learning. In this way, you can leverage the framework I will present here to guide you in cultivating an evidence-informed approach to learning that respects the past, reveres evidence for learning, and recognizes that learning is complex, non-linear, and adapting to context is essential.

What you do today with regards to the education of your children and the children you work with in your classroom is of monumental importance. Your choices of how to help students learn will influence the society's educational institutions and will have consequences. The Apostle, Paul, says in his letter to the Galatians: "Let us not become weary in doing good, for at the proper time, we will reap a harvest if we do not give up"[1]. A consistent message of wisdom throughout the Bible teaches that you reap what you sow. A Chinese proverb states similarly, "you reap what you sow – relationships, work, corn". Indeed, many cultures offer up the same sort of parable – that what is sown will, over time, bear harvest – however, the quality of that harvest depends significantly on the quality of the sowing and its continued maintenance.

There is no doubt that, in our current educational environment, there are many competing interests for how to have educators use our position of significant influence for competing causes. Some of these voices which will lead to good, some will be neutral, and quite frankly, many will be found detrimental. This book is designed to serve as a foundation from which any educator can be equipped with sufficient knowledge about the best of the old and the best of the new to help sow seeds that will bear bountiful fruit in the future.

Our current educational system, however, is one that has been aptly characterized as being lost in a wasteland of fads and buzzwords. There are very few professions that face as many claims of being "revolutionized" with as little change in practice as education. In an enlightening article on this very topic, Stephen Chew and William Cerbin (2007) satirically note that:

> If we were to synthesize current trends in pedagogy [teaching], we would conclude that the best teaching practice is: High impact, student-centered, engaging, hands-on, just-in-time, technology enhanced, flipped, blended, hybrid, transformational, cooperative, collaborative, reflective, authentic, situated, guided, integrative, supplemental, reciprocal, gamified, experiential, adaptive, disruptive and active. It is also brain-based, peer-based, inquiry-based, group-based, team-based, project-based, case-based, community-based, competency-based, evidence-based, mastery-based, research-based, service-based, problem-based, and data-driven, not to mention massive, open and online.[2]

Is it possible that all of this can be correct? Or, even if this synthesis were correct, could education truly encompass all of this in a coherent and feasible way? The answer to both is no. All of these are *not* correct with regards to effective pedagogy. Furthermore, even if they were, it is not possible to effectively integrate all of these into an educational program that leads to a coherent and successful learning environment. However, this certainly speaks to the daunting challenge teachers are tasked with on a daily basis: Given my students, their background knowledge, this particular point in time, their cohort, my knowledge base, standards that have to be met, and the time that we have, what is the best course of action? This is at the core of what teachers deal with every single day. It is unsurprising then, that many face burnouts and simply lose interest in the face of constant new demands given the basic needs we have to juggle each and every day.

Back to the point from Chew and Cerbin's satirical quote, though, any time you encounter something that is said to cause everything (or if you hear that everything is the cause of something), you can wager all your money that the truth is we lack the information to make any warranted conclusion and that various things are being mixed up in the diagnosis leading to such a wide range of claims. This satirical list of key ingredients in "best practices" for instruction simply underscores a real challenge for education in our day and age. Today's educational system is awash in a sea of buzzwords, driven by the latest fads, and increasingly prioritizes non-cognitive[3] measures of success, resulting in an environment that has largely lost touch with serious conversation with the enduring and influential ideas of the past. In many contexts, anything new is lauded as *innovative, creative, dynamic, engaging*, and so forth while virtually anything that has been done before is denigrated as *traditional*, which carries with it certain connotations of working in a factory assembly line. Is there any merit to this current synthesis of a lot of everything? Is "cutting-edge pedagogy" the key to unlocking learning? Are the ways of the past *passive*, completely *non-motivational*, and not worthy of use in planning your instruction? In this book, I will explain that the answer to each of these questions is a definitive *no*.

Ironically, the truth is that sometimes the most *progressive* person is not the one who continually marches forward on the path but the person who stops, walks back along the path to where it diverged and begins anew. When you take one step in the wrong direction, continuing on that path only leads you further away from where you want to be. Only in recognizing that something is wrong do we make the wise decision to not just take our foot off the accelerator but to use the brake, to slow down, and make a U-turn. In a case such as this, the one who turns back first is, in fact, the one who is the closest to real progress. Those who charge forward with every new educational fad in spite of evidence to the contrary do no favors to learners. However, this is not the only error. There are many on the opposite end of the spectrum guilty of a similar sin when it comes to improving ourselves. Those who refuse to consider relevant and well-done empirical research in our current age, simply because it is derived from our current age, are equally mistaken. Although the trends about what is best in education that I have quoted from Chew and Cerbin earlier are discouragingly accurate, there is also a good bit of sound educational research going on in education – in particular from the field of cognitive science. The growing base of empirical evidence from cognitive science to support particular principles of learning is perhaps the most important one for us to consider. And, intriguingly, its findings are not only things that do not contradict the good ideas from the past but rather reinforce them. This book presents my best efforts to walk back towards the path where we diverged and offer a measured and evidence-informed guide to where we ought to go now.

People in the past were not the ignoramuses that many of us imagine; nor were they muses infinitely wiser than we are today. We can learn from them, taking the best of what they developed while also considering the best evidence currently available to imagine real possibilities for broad, deep, rich, and meaningful learning. G.K. Chesterton used to say that every revolution is actually a restoration – the recapturing and re-application of something that once guided and inspired people in the past. I am convinced that in today's world what we need is not a transformational revolution to something entirely new. Rather, what is needed is a revolution akin to Chesterton's appeal – but one informed by the best currently available data rather than just a naïve hope to get back to the "good old days".

Education is one of the most influential and important responsibilities any society has. By recapturing the best elements of the past and applying them intentionally in our current context while seriously engaging with the best current evidence, we can lay foundations for an education that allows us to maximize our training of youth to equip them for success no matter what the future brings. It is in this way that I hope this book inspires you to act for your children's future. Embrace the tension between tradition and possibility and use this book to help build effective learning environments in your context.

Notes

1. Galatians 6:9 – translation from the New International Version.
2. A link to the full article, published online is here: https://www.insidehighered.com/views/2017/12/05/need-theory-learning-opinion
3. For instance, in many empirical studies researchers will downplay the importance of knowledge acquisition and instead place emphasis on affective measures such as: "grit", "growth mindset", "collaboration", and so forth. I do not suggest these are not valuable; I value each of them. But to prioritize those (affective measures) over learning (cognitive measure) is folly.

PART I
FOUNDATIONS
What Do We Need to Know?

1

Principles to Engage Learning

Learning is the most fundamental concept and purpose when it comes to education. Modern societies mandate education because it is assumed that by learning we can enhance our future. Learning is something that everyone believes that they know because we have all been in a classroom environment of some sort. Each of us thinks that this experience gives us insight into being able to "see" good instruction but this is a significant challenge as it dramatically undervalues the daunting challenge that is effective instruction. This perceived "knowing" about learning is highly deceptive because there is much more than meets the eye to effective instruction.

Within the scholarship on learning there are subtle issues that are helpful to know a little bit about. I don't think we need to be drawn into long debates about learning but we do need to at least begin with a baseline of factors that are acknowledged as elements required for learning. To establish this baseline, we will identify basic axioms – or principles – that are generally true and therefore of the most importance for us to know. These principles will not necessarily tell us what to do but they provide us an important filter through which we can then interact with specific strategies. The goal for the first two chapters will be to highlight some important preliminary considerations and then present six principles of how all of us learn that, if each teacher always kept in mind, would equip them to make decisions more likely to promote learning that lasts. So, let's begin with our brief dive into some preliminary information that is important to consider.

Learning seems to include at a very minimum the following requirements:

- Learning involves a change in a person's mind
- Learning requires an individual effort
- Learning fades but it can be lasting

These three key elements provide some important bounds to consider with regards to learning but they also leave some important things out. These things that are not addressed as a focal point herein ought to at least be acknowledged and briefly discussed so as to ensure they are not missed. Although they are not central to the purpose of this book, they are important to acknowledge, understand, and integrate into your effort to build effective learning environments. So, let us look at some preliminary issues related to learning before we explore the essential axioms.

Other Issues to Consider Related to Learning

In this section we will look at three specific issues we must consider before we dive into learning because each is related meaningfully to effective learning, yet each is distinct from it. These important issues include: The role of truth to learning; the relationship of learning to motivation; and the relationship of learning and values. This will serve as a prologue for our survey of learning principles.

The Role of Truth

A person can learn things that are correct and learn things that are incorrect. So, as persons committed to helping others learn we must commit to a few things to help ensure that learning is aimed in a positive direction. First, then, we must commit to the pursuit of truth. Learning ought to be considered "good" learning only insofar as it helps the learner learn things that are *true*. I have written an entire book on the problem of truth in education so let me distill the importance of this issue simply for the purposes in this book and I will encourage you to check out *The Decay of Truth in Education* for a more detailed account on why truth matters.

Anytime we are going to learn something it is right to ask: Why? And simply put, if we do not believe that what we are going to learn is most likely, based on the best evidence we currently have, to be objectively true then let's be honest, learning that is quite frankly just one's prerogative. Truth must be the prime aim for all learning. Truth serves as a lighthouse that does not get pulled with the turbulent winds of popular opinion. So, take some time to reflect on truth. If you believe each individual has their own truth then what you teach them does not matter. If so, the educator's job does not matter. The only thing that matters in that case is that each person believes whatever they prefer, and that they learn things that they want to learn. That is no recipe for a successful society as it will never engender any collective coherence. In fact, it is a recipe for chaos. Alternatively, if you believe that truth is just a construct used by the powerful to oppress others then you, as a person in a position of power, will see your role as one who must compel others to believe the "right things", which are those things that, of course, you believe. This is not a recipe for cultivating critical thinking but one for encouraging a propagandistic and dogmatic form of education.

So, we can see that truth is an essential topic to use as a lighthouse for learning. However, the principles I will discuss herein lead to learning – what we learn is not necessarily true and so this is one of the important issues educators must really think about. Are the learning experiences of your student(s) leading towards learning of things that are, based on the best evidence, true? Or, could their learning lead to all sorts of "learning" of falsehoods? The framework I will present herein will help ensure that student learning is long-lived and consequently, educators should seriously reflect on to what extent they are comfortable with students learning falsehoods and deliberately counteract such instances. Truth is monumentally important but it is a topic to be reflected on and used in conjunction with the principles of learning I will lay out ahead. So, for now, hold truth in high esteem as a target for our learners – we will explore this concept in more detail later.

The Relationship to Motivation

How motivated a person is to learn something can impact their learning. It is, however, not necessary to be motivated to learn. This is an important issue to lay out upfront because throughout this book my emphasis is on aspects related to learning; not related to motivation. Since I am not planning on spending a great deal of time on motivation I want to place emphasis on one key point for educators to know.

Motivation does not precede learning – rather successful learning precedes motivation. In fact, a longitudinal study ranging across elementary grades in a mathematics setting found that intrinsic motivation, at no time predicted student achievement but rather that prior achievement predicted subsequent intrinsic motivation (Garon-Carrier et. al., 2016). When learners get a taste of success, even in small bites, it builds up internal motivation to continue on. An effective educator, then, will build in opportunities to ensure small successes for your learner and leverage those for a lifetime of motivated learning rather than trying to get them motivated first. Success leads to motivation, not the other way around. As you work through this book and attempt to integrate its framework into your sphere of influence it would be wise to ensure you provide opportunities for success in your classroom to help students move towards intrinsic motivation rather than trying to build up motivation in its own right. Unless you are in a one-room schoolhouse or homeschool environment, trying to balance what motivates hundreds of different students is a waste of time. Focus on what will increase motivation of everyone – successful learning experiences. And do what you can to maximize potential opportunities for students to find success in your context.

The Relationship to Values
Knowledge about this or that is very difficult to learn without assessing some sense of whether or not '"x" is a good thing or a bad thing. Human beings are, by nature, prone to judge things. And contrary to popular opinion – judging ideas, actions, and so on – is a good thing. Take for instance the common way people point to the story of Jesus in the New Testament in which he is recorded to have said: "Do not judge, lest you be judged". Well, it's useful to look at that in its full context to make a proper interpretation of Jesus' exhortation:

> Do not judge lest you be judged. For in the way you judge, you will be judged; and by your standard of measure, it will be measured to you. And why do you look at the speck that is in your brother's eye, but do not notice the log that is in your own eye? Or how can you say to your brother, "Let me take the speck out of your eye" and behold the log is in your own eye? You hypocrite! First, take the log out of your own eye, and then you will see clearly to take the speck out of your brother's eye[1].

Notice that this biblical example frequently cited to claim we ought not to judge actually does the exact opposite when properly interpreted. Did you notice that the closing command is that you *should take the speck out of your brother's eye*? The point Jesus is making is that hypocritical judgment – criticizing another for something without acknowledging your own shortcoming – is in error. The point being made, properly understood, is that judgment is unavoidable and that we ought to judge considering our own brokenness and not from a position of unwarranted righteousness. When it comes to learning, there is constantly going to be inquiry into what is right and wrong. A traditional aim of education was development of virtuous citizens, which are defined as persons who think about good, the common good, and so forth. This is a good thing and you should actively work to cultivate reflection on the good, while you guide learners in the pursuit of truth, and inspire learners to live out their values consistently.

The Process of Learning

What you know determines what you see; it is not what you see that determines what you know. The importance of knowledge for learning cannot be understated. Learning is paradoxically predicated upon prior learning. The more knowledge one has the more they are able to learn. It is truly a case of the rich get richer. As an educator you should greatly value the knowledge that a learner is able to memorize because it will pave the way to more effective, enduring, and elastic learning in the future.

However, learning is not linear. We should not expect that once something is learned it is sufficiently stored in a person's mind that they can leverage it at their will. This is one of the reasons why review is so important. It is also a tacit endorsement for including some form of spiraling to your curriculum. Through a spiraling approach it necessitates learners to space out practice in domains, which is a method of improving learning that is empirically supported and will be expanded upon with a principle of learning on practice. Additionally, a spiraling approach allows you to dive deeper each time you spiral through similar content because retrieval of previously learned material is much quicker allowing for both broad and deep acquisition of knowledge. In this way it facilitates a meaningful transition of learner from novice in a domain towards expertise (not that expertise will be achieved during K-12 but it's a nice progression to look towards). Table 1.1 delineates some essential differences between novices and experts that should undergird our efforts to cultivate a learning environment for students who are, by their very nature, novices.

Some of the aspects of this table will be better clarified as we expand on the principles of learning but sufficed to say novices think in fundamentally different ways than do experts. If we want our students to move towards expertise it is not as simple as having them "do what experts do". As Ralph Waldo Emerson said, "every artist was first an amateur". Learning is not learned solely by embodying exactly what the expert does. It begins with knowledge acquisition, transitions towards application of knowledge in relevant skills, and moves towards interacting with ideas as experts do in the long-run.

The process of learning is, in effect, a slow and steady movement from pure novice towards expertise and undergoes many ups, downs, and important

Table 1.1 Novices versus Experts

Novices	Issue	Experts
Limited relevant knowledge	**Background Knowledge**	Extensive relevant knowledge
Working Memory	**Relies on during Learning New Material**	Long-Term Memory
Lacks an effective representation of successful performance	**Mental Representation of Success**	Has a clear representation of what success performance looks like
Requires clear steps or results in frustration	**Problem Solving**	Intuitive
Sees surface and superficial details	**What they "See"**	Sees underlying structures
Learn best through explicit instruction and worked examples	**How they Learn Best**	Learn best through discovery approaches
Struggles to transfer principles to new contexts	**Transfer**	Able to transfer principles between related contexts
Overloaded easily as attention is dominated by new information	**Working Memory**	Less likely to experience overload thanks to rich knowledge chunked in long-term memory

transitional points. In order to maximize effectiveness of learning for our students we should also have some guiding principles that enhance learning. In the remainder of this chapter I will outline a series of essential principles that you should know and apply in your context to improve the chances that learning will be maximized for your student(s).

Essential Principles to Enhance Learning

We have seen how there are important issues that relate to learning and can help us improve learning. We have outlined the process of learning and its non-linear nature. And finally, we have surveyed how expertise develops, which provides a crucial roadmap for what learning looks like in its highest forms. Having laid this out, I want to now present a set of essential principles of learning that are true for virtually all students. Consequently, you should consider each of these specifically in your context to help improve learning because they play a role for your students, too. Since chance favors the prepared mind by applying these principles in your context, you will be building a learning environment that ensures chance is favoring your learners.

These principles are derived from a systematic review and reflection on empirical investigations of learning over the past several decades. These principles are supported by the preponderance of the best evidence we have currently. These principles are true for virtually all learners in all circumstances. And finally, these principles are each relevant to any educator because considering them specifically can help learning and failing to abide by them hinders the learning process. Table 1.2 outlines the first three essential principles of learning that I have derived from this systematic review including a brief summary of each. Through the rest of Chapter One I will expand on each of these principles to describe each, to provide some specific research and/or evidence for each principle, and to offer specific ideas for how this should impact you as an evidence-informed educator. In Chapter Two, we will find three more principles. First, let us begin with a question: What is the essential condition for learning?

Table 1.2 Essential Principles to Engage Learning

Essential Principle of Learning	Brief Summary
Learning Requires Extended Thought	Learning involves a change that endures in an individual's mind. Learning is the "residue of thought" – the more a person thinks about something, the more that what is learned, endures.
Respect Cognitive Limits	Humans can only deal with limited "pieces" of non-memorized information at any given time. Learning is most effective when it respects these limits and intentionally equips learners to thrive.
Breadth of Essentials is Foundational	Learning is built upon prior knowledge. A breadth of essential information in a domain greatly enhances later and deeper learning by freeing up space in working memory to engage in such thought.

Principle #1: Learning Requires Time and Contemplation

The answer to that question on the essential condition is that *learning requires time and contemplation* – or put simply, *extended thought*. And this is our first axiom to engage learners effectively. This may, on its face, seem obvious but it is crucially important. Learning is an individual action and thus requires cognitive activity by an individual. And simply being exposed to something is not sufficient for learning to have occurred.

Take for instance, the hundreds and thousands of dimes you have held in your hands and pockets over the years. Whose face is on the dime? What about the image on the other side of the dime? What are all the words displayed on every coin, including the dime? Can you answer to each of those questions without looking at one? How about if you do look at a dime; does that help[2]? Or do you have to consult a device that can connect to the Internet to figure it out? If you would have to resort to looking it up online it is safe to say that you did not know it. In other words, something you have had immeasurable exposure to was still not something that you learned. And if you aced my example ask five other people; the odds are good that more than half will not know. The reason is quite simple; most of us don't really look at the dime and *think* about anything – except perhaps that its worth is ten cents.

Furthermore, simply playing with an idea is not sufficient for learning to endure. So, if you dive into Appendix A and read the page beginning to end (it's quite short) you have played with the idea and it will likely remain in your memory… for a time. However, unless you revisit this information, at various points, spread across time, the memory will fade and your learning will not endure. When you share this book with your friends we'll see just how much thought you put into the dime as they quiz you on the dime and you think, "darn it!".

You see, learning occurs in a person's mind through serious and sustained thought about something. This is not a thought that is mere casual interaction with an idea and moving on. Simply being exposed to an idea and working in a group project is not sufficient for such thought to lead to learning. Undoubtedly, the thoughts of the group will range wildly perhaps leading to a less likely case in which you will learn about your target. Such thought for learning is rarely achieved when sent aimlessly on the Internet to seek out information as we are bombarded with unnecessary information, vague information, dubious information, unrelated information, images – which may or may not be relevant, and tons of distractions (such as hyperlinks, pop-ups, and so forth). The fact that people can find things online gives them the illusion of knowledge. A wise person will stop using the Internet as a crutch and spend the time and focus necessary to learn information he or she wishes to know and store it in long-term memory so it is *their* knowledge.

That learning requires thought makes it deeply intentional. Learning requires focused, sincere, and sustained thought on a topic, which is why I use the word contemplation, which calls for extended, intentional thought. In order for you to actually learn something you need to think about it. You need to think about it sincerely and your thought should be both sustained and retrieved later on in many instances. Finally, it is very possible that we will *learn* things that are incorrect because it is very difficult to know what is in another person's mind – the only way we know is through asking them and getting a response in written or oral nature. There is no neuro-imagery machine that can tell us what our learners are thinking. No, nothing, except good old-fashioned Q and A. So, this principle is both critical and cautionary. We need our learners to think about what we want them to learn and we need to check what their thinking is focused on periodically during each lesson. If we fail to do so, they may be learning a great deal… of garbage.

How This Principle Should Impact Instruction

1 **Think carefully about what your learners will think about throughout each lesson**
    When you design your lessons – or choose a particular curriculum – think carefully about what students will be thinking about at each moment. At any given point when you do not know what learners are thinking about reflect on what your environment is cultivating. Does the lesson design require learners to stay focused on the task at hand throughout? If you cannot immediately respond to this question with a yes, consider ways you might be able to do so. You could simply add in some brief review questions throughout the lesson to reacquire their attention and refocus their thoughts to the goals at hand.
    And of course, be careful that you do not mix up too many intended learning outcomes resulting in an environment that is prohibitive towards learning. As an instructional designer it is your job to be sure the environment is not under-stimulating, nor over-stimulating. The key to this question is what is going on around the learner that will focus them and what will distract them – that will guide you to what they are likely to be thinking about.

2 **Provide meaningful opportunity to contemplate on learning**
    In today's society, people seem to be increasingly uncomfortable with silence. Do not allow such folly into your classroom. Require silence. Require reflection and contemplation. Give your children the opportunity to contemplate on the meaning of what was learned.

And then capitalize on it. Follow up by asking them about it – after their contemplation. This allows you to immediately take on any errors early on to refine the learners' thought so it is closer to true. Contemplation is a powerful tool in your arsenal for improving student learning.

Principle #2: Respect Cognitive Limits

So, what we are thinking about is the single best barometer for assessing what we will learn. Since we cannot see what others are thinking we need to keep them focused, ask them to explain their understanding and thought, and so forth. How much can a person think about at a given time is the next question we must consider because there is a bit of a bottleneck with regards to how our minds interact with information.

The second principle of learning is that *we must be aware of and respect cognitive limits*. First, we will begin with some essential background information. Cognitive science has provided some excellent research that is richly supported by empirical data showing that how our mind interacts with information has a certain flow to it. Basically, an individual (the learner) encounters information from their environment. One's environment can be filled with countless stimuli, each of which could draw their attention. As such, getting to what information is being encountered with begins with principle number one: What they choose to pay attention to. So, now the individual (the learner) chooses to direct their attention towards some (not all) of the available pieces of information while disregarding others. This is a process that is fairly complex in and of itself, and is a key reason why experts are so much better equipped to be bombarded with information than are novices. We'll explore that more in a later principle of learning.

At this point, we have barely moved from stage one (sensory memory) to stage two (working memory). The third stage of this flow of information is where "learning" truly occurs. As the individual (learning) selects information to focus on it becomes a focal point within that person's working memory. In order to begin the process of moving this information from working memory requires that the learner now begin to build connections with what is already stored in his or her long-term memory or works to simply memorize the information. I have constructed a visual representation of this flow through which information moves through our minds in Figure 1.1.

We have seen that there is a great deal of work going on within the mind as it interacts with the brain to 'process' information. But the process is just the background information you need to know to make sense of the principle. Now, the essential point we need to focus in on is working memory – the bottleneck in the learning process. The problem we face in learning is that

Principles to Engage Learning ♦ 13

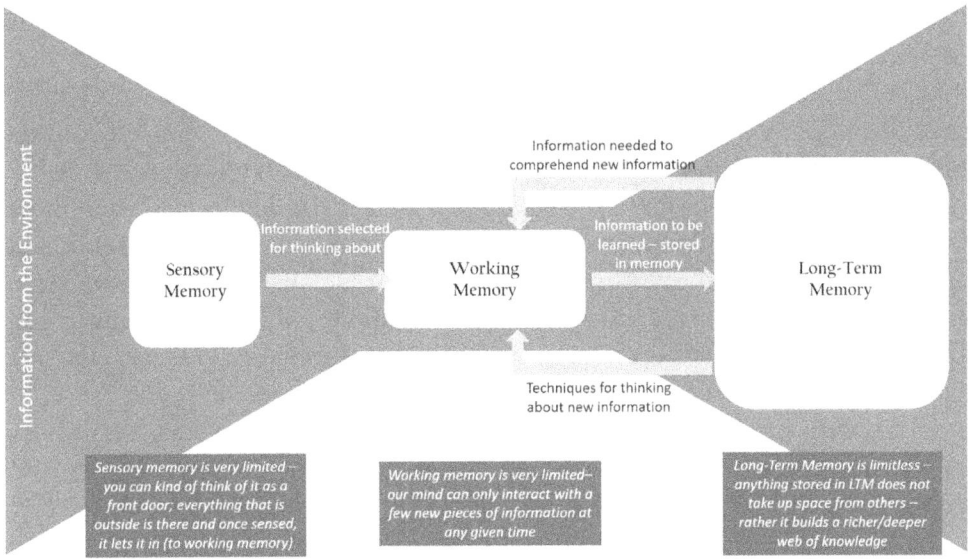

Figure 1.1 K's simplified model of the mind.

our working memory is more or less fixed – there is virtually nothing you can do to increase your working memory capacity significantly. In fact, perhaps unsurprisingly, for students with severe learning disabilities, it is almost always the case that their working memory capacity is significantly smaller than average. So, educators need to be aware of what this bottleneck's normal boundaries are so that they can design learning experiences that respect these cognitive limits.

Let's begin with a brief activity where you can experience the limits of working memory right now and in a few short pages we will revisit this and you can see how there is a silver lining for the educator who wants to overcome (work around is more like it) this bottleneck on the learning process. You're going to be on the honor system here for a moment so get ready for a quick quiz and be ready to just see what you can do. Look at Figure 1.2 for 10 seconds and then close the book and attempt to recite as many letters as you are able to state in the exact order in which they appeared.

The list from Figure 1.2 includes seven distinct units; each of which includes three different letters for a total of 21 distinct letters. For the most part, the trios should not include any that have meaning tied to them. What

K N C
A A F
B I C
I A U
S A A
C T M
L B K

Figure 1.2 Working memory activity.

researchers found was that when individuals were given activities such as this with meaningless information – which is, by definition, what any information that is new to us begins as – most people could recall around seven letters, plus or minus two. If you were above that, congratulations, you did well on assessment number one! If you were below that, just don't tell anyone… right? Just kidding. The point is that now you can get a sense of this process of how the mind interacts with information. Now, you could repeat this list again and again and again, and over time could do what is called rote memorization and memorize the units of meaningless information without understanding it. Don't! Please. It would be a waste of your time and soon you'll see why. There are good times to leverage rote memory; this list is not one of them!

The point from this activity is that this is a simulation of what is known as working memory and this is where the second principle really comes into play. When we encounter new information, our mind is only able to interact with and juggle a limited amount of information. And research has shown quite consistently that there are no real ways to make any significant change in our working memory space. Here is a very brief background on the research behind this mini experiment you just took part in.

Back in the mid-twentieth century, George A. Miller (1956) published a paper that has become something of a classic in cognitive psychology. His paper was entitled, *The magical number seven, plus or minus two: Some limits on our capacity for processing information*[3]. In this piece he built a fairly strong case for the fact that our working memory (the bottleneck I have referred to) can only handle seven, plus or minus two, distinct pieces of new information at any given time. Before getting excited that seven is the clear-cut magical answer you need it is important to note that more current research has actually rounded *down* Miller's number. Playing upon Miller's title, Nelson Cowan (2010) published an update to the research on working memory capacity and the title answers your question of: so what is the new number?! His piece was titled: *The magical mystery four: How is working memory capacity limited, and why*[4] and explained that the number is actually closer to four. So, how should the fact that our mind can only attend to a limited number of new ideas at any time impact our instruction?

There are two important take-aways from this significant limit to our cognitive capacity. First off, this number represents a very helpful specific range of items you should ask students to take on at any given minute (I'll have some good news for you soon on working around this limit). Secondarily, it must help you, as the educator who designs the learning environment, to focus yourself seriously on whether the lesson at hand includes a lot of unnecessary information or potentially distracting activity, and so forth that is actually hindering learner's working memory.

How This Principle Should Impact Instruction

1. **Be cautious about the number of steps you expect students to do without any instructor interaction**
   Often, students are given an assignment – or a collection of assignments/activities – and expected to use the time provided to complete the tasks given. This tactic may not be your wisest move given what we know about our limits to cognitive capacity. If you need learners to work for periods of time in which you cannot interact with them, ensure that there are clear stopping points and directions that do not require much effort to accurately interpret – or guessing what to do next. Because if they have to think about the directions that are new to them, that's minus one (assuming it's one-step to think about at a time) from their working memory and they're already at a handicap for achieving your learning aims.

2. **Be cautious about the types of activities you require students to do and be sure they are focused on the learning goal**
   Another critical area for the teacher to think about in this regard is the types of activities you are asking students to do. Working in groups can be very helpful; however, it can be extremely distracting and detrimental as well. Requiring students to create beautiful posters, presentations, and so forth to supplement an oral speech can be helpful; however, again, these can often distract both the one giving the presentation and those listening from the topic at hand by drawing their attention to multiple stimuli (stealing precious working memory space!) and linking back to our first principle we face an added possible problem. Not only does it reduce the space we can devote to learning the content, but it also changes what we are thinking about! If we spend forty minutes discussing backgrounds for our slides, images to use on our poster, and so on, with only twenty dedicated to focusing on the content of our speech, we've *thought about non-content material for over sixty percent of our learning time.* Back to the point at hand, respect the cognitive limits of your student(s) and help them maximize their potential for learning.

Principle #3: Breadth of Foundations Is Essential

Now we have established that what we actually think about is what we have a chance to learn. Additionally, we have seen that when it comes to dealing with "pieces" of information our mind has somewhat of a bottleneck in

K

NCAA

FBI

CIA

USA

ACT

MLB

K

Figure 1.3 Working memory activity, part II.

shuffling different things in terms of our limited space in working memory. What, then, can we do to reduce the limits of working memory on our minds to enhance learning?

The third principle in our list of essential principles for learning is that a *breadth of foundations if essential*. This is particularly important because, as I promised earlier, there is a way to work around the bottleneck limits of our cognitive capacity. In a simple phrase, it is called memorized factual knowledge. Let us revisit our activity from principle #2 in which you interacted with 21 letters but do so in the exact same order but with one slight twist. All right, we're about to go back on the honor system so, no cheating now! Same rules; look at Figure 1.3 this time for 10 seconds and then close the book and attempt to recite as many as you are able to state in the exact order in which they appeared.

How did you do this time? Better, I suspect! The word that is in play here with regards to learning is called "chunking". The letters were presented in the exact same order. The only distinction was that I chunked them differently – in particular, I did so in ways that you probably already had information stored in your long-term memory about giving meaning to the list and allowing you to do much better. This activity has now helped you in contextualizing both principle number two – that our ability to think has limits and should not be overburdened – and also principle number three – that we can work around those limits by placing relevant information into long-term memory. Now, memorizing everything is simply too time consuming to make sense, unless you've got a photographic memory. And that is why I said it would be a waste of your time to memorize the list from earlier. So, I have phrased the principle of learning intentionally to address that. Notice that I have focused this principle to not merely memorize everything but hitting the areas that are best able to be leveraged for future learning: A broad base of foundations (essentials) for each and every domain.

Your learners, if equipped with a broad base of foundational knowledge, stored in long-term memory will be able to use that information as they encounter other information at *zero cost to their working memory capacity!* This is that wonderful work-around I noted earlier. Advocates of classical learning have long argued that memorization of basic factual information is critically important. More recently, many cognitive scientists have empirically demonstrated the exact same thing. For instance, the importance of providing broad knowledge early in one's education is illustrated by Hannust and Kikas (2007) who, in an investigation of children's knowledge of astronomy, found that: "Children acquire factual information rather easily and therefore early instruction should introduce the core facts related to the topics" (p. 89) A wise teacher will ensure that he or she helps his student(s) memorize the foundational information for a particular domain, class, unit, and so on because a broad foundation of essential knowledge is foundational to deeper and longer-lasting learning.

How This Principle Should Impact Instruction

1 **Identify foundational (essential) information for learning in your domain**
   This implication should be recognized as being scalable. That is, the teacher should really clarify what the necessary foundational information of a course/unit/lesson/topic is and specifically build in plans to help his or her learners memorize that information early on in the process. In doing so, it will free up working memory as learners begin engaging in more difficult tasks. This would include things such as math facts (multiplication tables), a general chronology of human history (timeline from beginning to the present), and so on.

2 **Use memorization strategies to help guarantee learners are equipped with a broad foundation of knowledge**
   There are various strategies that have a good track record for actually improving a students' ability to memorize such key information. Using songs, stories and mnemonic devices, for example, can be great ways to help learners memorize this foundational knowledge in your context. Using stories – or a story form – to convey information is a fantastic strategy to utilize to enhance learning (Egan, 2005). Cognitive psychologists call stories "psychologically privileged" because our minds seem intuitively designed to remember them better than other forms of text (Bower, 1978; Graesser, Singer, & Trabasso, 1994; Willingham, 2004). So, if appropriate, see if you can present content in a story form where characters are introduced, a conflict emerges – including an adversary to overcome, exposition builds up to a climax when the conflict is resolved, and then the story unfolds to its conclusion. This can't be used in all circumstances, but when it can, don't hesitate to tap into it; your student's mind(s) seem predisposed to engage with them.
   Second, use mnemonic devices such as acronyms and acrostics. Do you recall PEMDAS or ROY G BIV? Both are mnemonic devices

that can help learners memorize essential information. PEMDAS is an acrostic that stands for *Please Excuse My Dear Aunt Sally*, a sentence that exists solely as a device to help learners remember the letters in the correct order so that they can properly compute mathematical problems in the correct order of operations – P (parenthesis), E (exponents), M (multiplication), D (division), A (addition), and S (subtraction). ROY G BIV does not have any sentence accompanying it so it is an acronym in which students recall the acronym itself so they can memorize the order of the colors in the rainbow – R (red), O (orange), Y (yellow), G (green), B (blue), I (indigo), and V (violet). Such mnemonic devices are wonderful tools to use when appropriate to help memorize foundational information.

Summary

This first chapter explores the very foundations for how learning works and how we can leverage this evidence to inform our practice. We began by considering topics beyond just principles of learning and reflected on our ultimate aim being the pursuit of truth for learning things that are untruthful is not helpful and so we need to step back and think about ensuring what we learn is, based on the best currently available evidence, true. We also discussed the role of motivation and noted that since our students have many differing interests and desires the best motivational tool to leverage is success – build in wins for your students to cultivate their motivation rather than trying to appease everyone. We also affirmed that a consideration of what is right and wrong, good and evil, and so forth is a healthy thing we want to engage students in while learning. With these broad affirmations we began our survey into clarifying essential axioms about learning that ought to inform our practice. In this chapter we focused on principles to engage learning. I have articulated three of those:

- Learning requires time and contemplation
- Learning is most efficient when we respect cognitive limits
- Learning a broad foundation of knowledge is key to "deeper" or "higher" thinking

Next, we will continue our survey of essential principles that ought to guide our practice by exploring principles that extend learning. Before moving ahead, take time and contemplate on what you have just interacted with.

Here are a few ideas for reflection and application and after you think on those, I'll see you in the next chapter!

For Reflection and Application

Thinking back on this chapter, consider the following reflective tasks and ideas for application in your classroom:

1. What are two-to-three takeaways from this chapter for your practice as an educator?
2. What is one thing you can do tomorrow to immediately put these principles into practice?
3. Commit these principles to memory so that when you make your hundreds and even thousands of decisions a day, they are with you to help narrow the scope of possibilities to those most likely to engage learning

Notes

1. Matthew 7:1–5, translated from the New International Version of the Holy Bible.
2. For those who need to know now, I have provided a short one-pager of information in Appendix A. Enjoy but if you want to know this, be sure you *think about it*, and beyond just right now, because as you'll see in the next moment – playing with an idea in one moment does not mean it will endure!
3. The article is listed in the references and includes a direct link for reading in its entirety online if you'd like.
4. The article is listed in the references and includes a direct link for reading its entirely online if you'd like.

2

Principles to Extend Learning

In Chapter One we laid the first foundation for our framework on learning by establishing some general understandings and clarifying three axioms for how learning works with an emphasis on principles to engage learning. In this chapter we will add a second foundation for our framework on learning by looking at three additional axioms for how learning works. This time our emphasis will be placed on principles that extend learning. Table 2.1 presents the next three principles of learning derived from a systematic review of the current body of research on learning.

Essential Principles to Extend Learning

Just as the three principles to engage learning have been derived from a systematic review and reflection on the empirical literature, this is also true for the three principles to extend learning that we will look at in Chapter Two. Each of these axioms is supported by the preponderance of best current evidence and they are true in virtually all learning contexts. This is important. People often say (or think), well this doesn't make sense in my context but for these systematically derived principles that is largely untrue. The proper response to this is: Yes, context matters. But to deny the benefits of applying these principles because of "context" is intellectually shallow. Can you explain any context in which this principle is no longer relevant? The list of possibilities for in which they would not apply is incredibly small and

Table 2.1 Essential Principles to Enhance Learning

Essential Principle of Learning	Brief Summary
Knowledge First; Then Skill	Effectively deploying skills and applying information requires accurate understanding first. Ensure requisite knowledge is in place before jumping into application and skill activities.
Practice: Deliberate, Spread, and Varied	Becoming skillful at anything requires extended practice. Certain types of practice are more effective for learning. Spread out practice, vary the challenges during practice, and ensure that feedback is provided from experts to coach learners to refine specific knowledge/skills.
Learning Early and Late are Significantly Different	When we are new to a domain we learn in fundamentally different ways than experts do. Don't have learners mimic what experts do; instead, learners need much guidance and time to build a broad/rich knowledge-base. As one moves towards expertise they need less guidance.

virtually never going to be the case in any typical classroom environment. So, keep these principles in mind – all the time. They do not tell you exactly what to do, but filtering all the possibilities through them will help you discern more efficiently between actions that will hinder versus those that will help build effective learning environments.

Principle #4: Knowledge First; Then Skill

The first thing we explored to reduce the limits of working memory on our minds is to ensure that learners are equipped with a broad base of essential content knowledge in any domain. From that frame of reference, the student is able to use that high-leverage (highly used) knowledge at no cost to his or her working memory. But that is not the only thing we can consider with regards to reducing the limits of working memory on our minds. This leads us to our fourth principle of learning.

The fourth principle of learning is that *knowledge should be built first and then skill should be developed*. For years educators have argued about whether knowledge or skills should be the priority for learning. The suggestion that these are somehow at odds is nonsense[1]. However, there should be a sequential order in most cases through which learning will be maximized: (1) Build the background knowledge to help the learner first and (2) practice the skills associated with the task afterwards.

This sequence is important for a variety of reasons. First, knowledge literally builds upon other knowledge. In other words, there is a reciprocal relationship between background knowledge and ability to engage in higher order thinking tasks; those who bring less to the table are significantly limited and likewise, those who bring more are significantly privileged. As we saw earlier, having a broad knowledge base (principle #3) increases the likelihood that learners encountering new information can have information to pull from their long-term memory (retrieval) and connect new ideas to.

This brings us to a helpful analogy to consider for our mind operates. A good way to think about how your mind organizes information is like a spider web; ideas and knowledge that are more well-understood by an individual stand firmly in the middle of the web. These ideas are deeply entrenched making them (a) harder to change and (b) easier to make meaningful connections to other ideas[2]. However, this fact also has potential consequences. The problems that result from this is that if a learner spends a great deal of time learning things that are wrong, it is harder to change them because those false ideas are deeply woven into their web of understanding. So, it is all the more important that teachers check student understanding and help them correct misconceptions early on so they don't have to deal with deeply entrenched falsehoods. You may have heard that failure is good for learning. I agree insofar as we are talking about the fact that students need to understand they will not always be successful. But if you believe that more failure produces better learning, that is extending the benefits of failure well beyond reality. Furthermore, for a teacher to allow their students to fail in a setting where they could have avoided it will lead to decreases in students' motivation and self-esteem. Jean Twenge (2014) explains the foolishness of those who have believed that the correction of mistakes is a threat to their self-esteem:

> Another facet of this movement says that teachers should not correct children's mistakes, lest this hurt their self-esteem. This is extremely misguided: Children learn by having their mistakes corrected, and their self-esteem is hurt when they later find out that they've been doing something wrong for years and aren't prepared. (223)

The fact that our mind organizes information into what you might imagine as a web of knowledge is, thus, of critical importance. The more knowledge one has, the stronger their web will be (more threads), the more interconnected their understanding is, the stronger their web will be (more overlapped knowledge), and the more coherent one's understandings are the more easily they will be able to live and apply their values in day-to-day life consistently. All of these are benefits from this structural analogy I have provided for how our mind organizes information. So, how does this structure of knowledge help when it comes to skill development?

By ensuring that learners are equipped with sufficient background knowledge before jumping into application you will find that they are much more apt to respond to the nuances that come with doing. I am a big fan of the old military adage that the best laid plans never survive first contact with the enemy. This dovetails neatly here. When we start to try out a new skill, invariably we will encounter bumps in the road that the instructor may not have thought to be immediately relevant – why? Because you can't teach everything before diving in! But, having some background knowledge in place allows the learner to interact with the challenges of implementation far more successfully than they would by blindly playing with the skill. You could think of this in line with a quote often attributed to Benjamin Franklin: "By failing to prepare you are preparing to fail". If we fail to prepare our minds with the knowledge necessary to apply skills in a domain, we are preparing to fail in our efforts to engage in the skills.

How This Principle Should Impact Instruction

1   **Avoid pure discovery methods of instruction most of the time**
    Because our mind organizes information into these webs of knowledge, the best-case scenario for learners is typically to receive significant amounts of guidance early, tapering off over time as they become more competent in a domain. Pure discovery methods of instruction not only have a terrible track record (Mayer, 2004) but also make little sense in light of this principle. Knowledge should precede skill and consequently, wise teachers will avoid pure discovery unless they are working with students whose knowledge is so rich that they are closer to experts (real experts, like Dr. House from Fox's old TV series; not emerging experts like a first-year doctor who has completed his/her entire medical training – that person has years and years of deliberate practice to go before they will achieve real expert status).

2   **Ask questions after students have been exposed to background information to promote good thinking**
    Often, people find it engaging to ask a provocative question at the outset of a lesson before any information about a phenomenon is known. However, having students spend time dwelling on

something that they lack sufficient background knowledge to think about it is not a very efficient use of time. It would be far wiser to hold off on that particularly compelling question so that, when posed, it is compelling not just because it is provocative but because the learner actually sees what makes it interesting. That requires knowledge to see and having that knowledge already in place, the learners can then skillfully engage with it and attention can be more meaningfully captured. Additionally, by asking these questions after building knowledge we help ensure that we are equipping all our students equally. The unequal access to knowledge creates power imbalances in groups – and this relates directly to how much power they have to apply the relevant skills enhanced by that knowledge.

3 **Be cautious of technology if it becomes a crutch for building knowledge**

Many people in today's technologically-infused world erroneously devalue the role of building knowledge, instead thinking devices and the Internet can accomplish basic factual knowledge. Nothing could be further from the truth. It would be wise for you, as an educator, to significantly limit the use of technology as a crutch for not memorizing basic factual knowledge. Maryanne Wolf (2018), in a book that looks at how technology has altered how our mind operates[3] explains: "Our increased reliance on external forms of memory, combined with the attention-dividing bombardment by multiple sources of information, is cumulatively altering the quality and capacities of our working memory" (p. 82). Adhering to this principle is an important step in fighting against this unavoidable challenge our learners face in the digital age by intentionally committing to build knowledge and make it our learners own before jumping into application.

Principle #5: Practice – Deliberate, Spread, and Varied

So far, we have seen that the essential condition for learning is *thought* – we have the potential to learn only what we think about. We saw that we are limited cognitively and that good educational design will take those limits into consideration so as to not overload learners. Next, we saw that by ensuring learners commit to memory a broad base of foundational knowledge in a domain and by making sure knowledge is in place before skills are applied can help reduce the limits imposed on cognition by working memory. Now, we have some general frame of reference for the overall process of learning, which leads us to our next question: What can we do to make learning last?

The fifth principle of learning is that *in order to achieve expertise – or mastery – in any domain requires practice. And not just any type of practice, but practice that is deliberate, practice that is varied, and practice that is spread over time.* Each of these descriptors is important and derived from empirical research that demonstrably improves retention of learning.

Let us begin with the overall principle. It is important to note that when referring to practice we are specifically referring to something that has been learned and is now being used. In the classroom, this means that you are practicing something you have already learned. We should not learn something once and then move on to never view it again – to do so is to guarantee that it will fade quickly and soon be forgotten. But simply repeating the same thing again and again is not going to push learners towards continual improvement, which is what we're focusing on here. Effective practice is deliberate, spread across time, and varied in form. Let's now explore what each of these descriptors looks like specifically.

Effective practice is deliberate. K. Anders Ericsson and his team of researchers out of Florida State University have studied expertise in many domains, including sports. One of the defining characteristics they found of experts in each domain was that they took part in sustained periods of time in which they engaged in what they coin: *Deliberate practice*. Deliberate practice is purposeful and systematic. It is more than simply repetition, although repetition is part of it. Deliberate practice requires focused attention, getting feedback from someone knowledgeable, and practicing with the intent to improve performance. There are four essential components of deliberate practice:

1 The learner must be motivated to focus on the task and exert effort to improve performance
2 The task should be designed based on your prior knowledge
3 The learner should receive immediate feedback regarding their performance and how to improve
4 The task should be repeatedly performed

If you're paying attention you might notice that some of the features of deliberate practice are not necessarily going to be something students will choose. They require motivation to *improve* – that means the learner probably needs to want to get better at "x" subject or "y" task. Points 2 and 3 together means that the task is likely going to stretch the learner and provide corrective feedback to improve them, which virtually ensures it's not just an easy practice task. And repetition is good for making things more entrenched in our minds but not necessarily good for motivation. In other words, applying deliberate practice is probably not something you can do all the time – rather, I would advise you be intentional about the most essential areas in your domain and see if you can integrate opportunities to engage in deliberate practice in those areas.

In addition to effective practice being deliberate there are also a few other strategies that are strongly supported by empirical research that lead to improved learning. Practice that is spaced out over time is better for long-term learning than is practice that is crammed in the night before it is needed. *Spaced practice* takes the amount of time you might have spent cramming and spreads it out across a much longer period of time. So, if you spread out your practice on something you are preparing for (say the ACT) and spread out your practice for it over the course of a month, it will lead to longer lasting learning of the material than if you packed all the practice in right before the ACT (or whatever else you are preparing for). I should also clarify that we're talking about the same amount of study time. If you were going to cram for four hours, spread those four out across weeks and the learning will *endure longer*. Of course, spreading it across time does allow for you to study more, which would also be beneficial but the point I want to make clear for us is the same amount of study time, spread out, will work better for learning that lasts than will the same amount of time done right before a performance[4].

One final element of effective practice that leads to long-term learning is varying its form and what it is mixed in with (called *interleaved practice*). In effect, this means that the best types of practice are not simply redoing the exact same motion or task again and again without any changes in between but rather ones that require the learner to shift their attention to topic A and back to topic B, and so forth. For example, as a golf coach of nearly a decade I was blessed with some wonderful talent and good luck (I didn't know anything about the information in this section at the time but employed it because it seemed right to me even if I didn't know it actually was right!). One of the methods we would do was focus on our short game (roughly speaking within 100 yards of the green). A typical golfer who chooses to practice on this[5] type of skill will pick a spot and drop a pile of balls hitting the same shot repeatedly until the balls are gone and then move to another spot. However, if I am to do *interleaved practice* I am going to vary the form of what I am doing between attempts. When coaching I would have about eight spots set up ranging across forty yards – at approximately 5–10-yard intervals (see Figure 2.1 for a visual depiction of this). Typically, this meant that each shot would be slightly to moderately different than the one before it. Rotating through required the athletes to recall the swing path and motion not simply from what had been immediately prior to it. This is an example of interleaved practice in action.

Figure 2.1 Coach K's interleaved practice at golf.
Background Image from Creative Commons
"Backyard Golf Hole" by John Beagle is licensed with CC BY 2.0. To view a copy of this license, visit https://creativecommons.org/licenses/by/2.0/

The athletes would hit one shot at their designated spot and then would move to a new spot. You will notice that the spots vary in their distance to the hole. Additionally, they also vary in their form – some are best suited for a chip (a lower shot that will land and roll out) while others are best suited for a pitch (a higher shot that will land and stop quickly). During practice, we would frequently have practice sessions such as these, which leads to better long-term learning. However, and this is *important*, in the moment they are *harder*! My athletes would have preferred to hit twenty shots in a row at each location because they would do better in the moment. But luck was with me as I held firm and used this model as a frequent practice tool. We were able to take the immediate feedback of (a) our ability to judge distance, (b) our ability to determine how long our backswing should be for each and the best launch angle for the ball to release towards the hole, (c) replicate practice as it would be in the real games (mulligans are not allowed in tournament golf!), (d) and I was right there to work with each of them on specific issues that arose with each of them. Over the long-term, practice that is varied – or interleaved – in a model such as this leads to richer, more sustained learning. It is, however, harder in the moment so don't expect it to be preferred by your learners unless they are strongly motivated to learn for the sake of learning!

As an important related comment, don't let student preference dominate your classroom. Learning is kind of like feeding your brain. In what sense would it be rational to say that I will let my child choose what food he or she eats because it is what he or she prefers? In my case, my parents wisely told me "**no,** you cannot eat candy all the time; you have to eat your vegetables" (in fact, my wife still does so…). If certain foods are better for you than others, wiser persons should force you to include some healthy ones. The same is true for learning – often what is preferred is not what is best. Often it is preferred because it is "easiest". Unfortunately, what is "easiest" typically leads to the shallowest and weakest learning; learning that is less likely to endure. The teacher is much closer to an expert than the learner is and having read this, you are much more likely to know what is best for them than they are. Let your preference for effectiveness of learning overrule their preference for ease of learning.

How This Principle Should Impact Instruction

1 **Ensure that you provide time every single day for review of past material**

    Effective instruction begins with a review of past material daily to both contextualize new learning but also, and perhaps more importantly, to solidify past learning. Ensure that your learners have ample time built into their day to review what they have learned. Provide time for reflection and discussion spread across the day – not necessarily immediately during learning – and encourage your student(s) to apply the principles of *deliberate* and *spaced practice*.

2 **Do not stop reviewing simply because someone seems sufficient at it**

    When a person has done something well enough to do it right one time is the exact wrong time to give it up! Again, I find sports as a useful analogy – probably because I have been involved in them professionally nearly as long as I have in the classroom. I had the honor of playing baseball through high school and into college. And guess what I practiced every single day from the first day I hit the field until I was playing as a teammate at Arizona State University with future major leaguers[6]? We practiced throwing the ball, catching the ball, and fielding ground balls. I was, by most accounts, a very strong defensive player and yet I worked day after day after day on ground balls to increasingly refine my skill all the way through division-I college baseball. Don't let your students stop doing something just because they have done it well before. Spread out opportunities to revisit the skill or knowledge over time or work on more precise work on essentials so that rather than fading out, their learning endures.

Principle #6: Learning Early and Late Is Different

We have now surveyed the essential conditions for learning, limits to our ability to interact with information, tools to help overcome the challenge of those limits, and now we have looked at what leads to enduring learning. This seems like a pretty good overview but there is one last, and very important, question: What else should an educator know to enhance, extend, and maximize learning?

The last principle of learning that I want to emphasize in this book is that *how learning occurs looks fundamentally different early in development and late in development in a domain.* This final principle is in some ways integrative of all former principles. That is because it, distinguishes between what learning looks like for novices (what are students are) and experts. The distinctions are dramatic between them. Even the differences between experts and near-experts are significant.

The level of knowledge one has in any domain is the critical factor in determining what information they focus in on when encountering a problem. Take for example; a medical doctor who is an expert and a team of doctors-in-residence (completed all education, now in training). The doctors are bombarded with information and while both expert and near-experts have similar knowledge-bases, the way the information is organized in the expert's mind is qualitatively different. This is not something that happens by luck – it happens through adhering to principles one-through-five long enough in a particular domain that one becomes a true expert. At this point, what happens is that they are able to see the *deep-structure* of problems that are encountered. Even the near-experts are more likely to focus on issues that are on the surface possibly important but that miss the deeper structure involved. Novices, unlike the expert and near-expert lack adequate knowledge and thus will focus only on the surface issues and become very easily distracted by irrelevant information because they have no filter to determine what is of consequence and what is superficial. Experts are best able to learn through engaging in problem solving of especially challenging issues that work in this "deep structure" area. Novices, however, will flounder and fail on such tasks because they lack the knowledge necessary to get to the "deep structure". Novices thrive when learning through direct instruction as opposed to unguided discovery and the expert's ability to learn well in unstructured domains while not being helped by direct instruction has been coined the expertise reversal effect (Kalyuga, Ayres, Chandler, and Sweller, 2003).

What does all this mean in terms of learning? It means that when you are working with students you must consider where they stand developmentally in the domain. For virtually all students (K-12) the fact of the matter is that they are novices. In other words, don't have students play the role of experts if you want them to learn content. "Doing history" and "Doing Science" can be fun and there is nothing wrong with doing it, however, having them do this as a means for learning content is not going to be nearly as productive as virtually any other format. So, expose your students to lab experiments, engage them in writing of historical arguments, and so forth, but do so to expose them to the processes these disciplines operate by not to learn material. The learners will be focused on the processes at hand but they lack the knowledge to effectively do what they are supposed to and any learning that occurs will be far less impactful than they would have through a direct model. Use these to introduce learners to the processes in a domain and perhaps to check information they have already mastered but don't expect it to lead to rich knowledge.

I work with PhD and EdD students and had a conversation with a leading cognitive scientist on this (Dan Willingham) and in our discussion he stated: "The novice status is true for most graduate students, too". So, it is not terribly helpful to imagine that your child, or your students, are experts. Expertise is not something developed in a short time. Furthermore, it is not possible without applying extended practice, developing broad and deep knowledge, receiving helpful corrective feedback and coaching, serious inquiry, sincere reflection, and extended thought.

Your student(s) are novices in virtually all cases so you should ensure that you provide them sufficient guidance and scaffolds if you want to maximize their learning. In the cases where they begin to be more developed in certain domains you may start considering including some more inquiry-oriented lessons but not so much because it will help them learn content but more because it will engage them in practices that experts engage in. The shift towards including more application type activities is one that makes sense only in light of a strong background knowledge already being in place.

How This Principle Should Impact Instruction

1 **Provide ample guidance, worked examples, and corrective feedback to learners**

    Because in virtually all cases your student(s) are novices it is particularly important that you integrate learning strategies that have been demonstrably shown to be effective for their learning. This includes first and foremost, guidance. The teacher is far closer to an expert-status in the domain than is the student – consequently, the teacher should identify areas that are best suited to provide guidance for learners. Imagine a grand-scale *gradual release* model for each domain in which the learner begins with significant guidance and that guidance tapers off over time. Provide *worked examples* to students as this is another of the most well-documented strategies for improving learning. A worked example is an already completed problem provided for the learner to reference while working on such problems. Studies have found that providing students fewer problems to complete themselves and a few worked examples leads to better learning than does more problems completed by themselves (Atkinson, R.K., et. al., 2000; Chen, Kalyuga, and Sweller, 2016). Finally, it is essential that the teacher provide feedback to students on their progress. Bruce Tulgan (1999) offers a helpful mnemonic for remembering key aspects of effective feedback: F.A.S.T. feedback. That means that corrective feedback should be Frequent (F), Accurate (A), Specific (S), and Timely (T). Be sure to build in opportunities to provide such feedback to your learners – it is an essential element for moving them towards expertise.

2 **As learners become more advanced in a domain, allow them to engage in more discovery-oriented and creative opportunities**
   Students in their K-12 experience are not going to become real experts in almost anything (research on this suggests it takes approximately ten full years of deliberate practice[7] so this is not an attack against the kids; it's a statement of fact with regards to the nature of expertise). However, when students have acquired sufficient background knowledge allowing them to engage in some forms of inquiry and/or creative expression are worthwhile endeavors that can also enhance learning. For example, having students who have a rich knowledge of a subject create a visual display to depict it will be beneficial to their learning. Such an activity would be mostly non-productive for those early in learning a domain.

Summary

Learning is the single most important issue when it comes to a person's education. It is the primary aim of our studies whether our aim is learning about history, science, mathematics, grammar, art, God, and so on. Over the past several decades research in cognitive science has made significant transitions in understanding how we come to learn information. In Chapters One and Two I presented six principles of learning distilled from that research. Each of these principles is so strongly supported by the research that they form a baseline of essential axioms that educators ought to consider when teaching and learning in any context.

For Reflection and Application

Thinking back on this chapter, consider the following reflective tasks and ideas for application in your classroom:

1. What are 2-to-3 takeaways from this chapter for your practice as an educator?
2. What is one thing you can do tomorrow to immediately put these principles into practice?
3. Commit these principles to memory so that when you make your hundreds and even thousands of decisions a day, they are with you to help narrow the scope of possibilities to those most likely to engage learning

Notes

1. One cannot apply skill effectively without knowledge and to know things without putting them into action in any way seems to be a waste. Consequently, we should dismiss such attempts to view knowledge and skills as separate – they are intertwined, necessarily. However, knowledge should precede skill to maximize learning.
2. This is true not only for knowledge, but also for our beliefs. The beliefs that are more firmly entrenched in our worldview are ones we are less likely to change on when encountering information that challenges our beliefs (this is one reason that all those on radical ends of the spectrum politically are so predisposed to confirmation bias about ideas related to politics.
3. I should note that a great deal of these impacts seem to be detrimental to our mind although Wolf does not advocate for its complete removal. It is a great book, I highly recommend to read: *Reader, come home*.
4. I would be remiss if I did not also note that cramming immediately before a test has shown to be more effective for immediate benefits, but that the

learning from such an approach is shallow and lost quickly. Which is why, even the next day you are surprised you have forgotten things it seemed like you had mastered – quickly in, quickly out!
5. And they are hard to find anyway as most would prefer to just play the course or perhaps spend fifteen minutes bombing as many drives off the practice tee as they can. Does that sound like you? Increasingly, it does to me too; these days… perhaps I've lost my focus for improving as a golfer.
6. Future major leaguers insofar as we are contextualizing this to my time in college. At the time of writing this book, Dustin Pedroia is a current major leaguer and is nearing the end of his career so perhaps he is retired by now as you read this. In any case, context is the key to determining meaning of a passage so I've clarified it for this one!
7. K. Anders Ericsson is the leading scholar in the study of the nature of expertise and his 2016 book, *Peak*, is a wonderful resource in this regard. Gladwell (2018) popularized some of the findings in *Outliers*, but Ericsson's work is better in my opinion.

3

Learning Myths and Other Nonsense

Thus far we have placed emphasis on understanding basic truth – or axioms or principles – about how people learn generally so that we can keep those in mind as we juggle our many decisions each day. Now we will take a short detour to explore some of the more widespread erroneous beliefs that are found in education. As Mortimer Adler has said of engaging with the great books, "some basic truths are to be found… but many more errors will also be found there, because a plurality of errors is always to be found for every single truth". In interacting with an applied field with as many goals as education has this point is undoubtedly true, as well, and so we will look at common myths and nonsense that we ought to be aware of so that they do not negatively influence our ability to build effective learning environments.

I encourage you, as I do all my students, to commit to embracing the principles we previously reviewed but also through seriously engaging in critical analysis of ideas we hold that may be, in fact, false. So, imagine this chapter as a quick application of logic in which we will examine some commonly held myths about learning and destroy poor arguments and other nonsense peddled in today's world of education.

Myths about Learning

Before we take the bold claim as to say we believe that we have an idea worth pursuing it is equally important to survey the landscape and identify any folk lore that we may believe that is actually dubious. If we are to preach that rich knowledge about domains, careful reasoning, and articulate expression are the foundational elements from which our curricula will be formed ought we not clean house through some critical reasoning of our own? In this section I want to examine three myths that are widely believed. And if we truly want to build effective learning environments from which we become masters in the art of learning then we must be willing to take the scalpel to our own views and cut off beliefs that we may hold that do not pass the test of reason and evidence.

Myth 1: Learning Styles Matter

Everyone learns in their own unique way. True. Everyone has preferred means of learning. True. You can accurately identify a learner's preferred learning style and by teaching to that you will improve learning. False.

This opening series of statements is deliberate and important. Might learning styles exist for learners? Sure. But does it really help a child's learning ability if you identify them as "kinesthetic" or "auditory" and teach them in that manner? No. The bottom line for learning is that people are actually more alike than different in terms of how they make sense of information. And when it comes to learning, what is important is not personal preference but coherence. A "kinesthetic" lesson in mathematics might at times make sense – for example, to help provide a concrete example for fractions with pizza slices. However, that has almost nothing to do with the individual learner; it has, instead, to do with the learning objective. *The content or skill to be learned should be your driving force for deciding whether or not a particular style of instruction is appropriate – not a learner's preference.* Consider an analogy: All people also have food preferences. Mine is for Coke and Steak. Would it help me to always provide me nutrition in my preferred ways? Of course not! In the case of learning, it is equally true. Our preferences may fit with what is best for reality; or they may not. In any account, as a person who is leading learning you should use your expertise to determine what is most appropriate for the content and skill to be learned and *not* what is most preferable to the learner.

There is a significant difference between how we believe we prefer to learn and what actually leads to better learning. Ample research has been done on learning styles and their application for improving learning and the bottom line is that, at best, teaching to a students' preferred learning style has no impact – in some cases, it is negative. Way back in 1982, Richard Clark found that learner preference was typically uncorrelated or negatively correlated with learning and learning outcomes. More comprehensively, Pashler et al. (2008) surveyed the empirical literature on learning styles and again noted the same thing. Teaching to a persons' self-identified preferred learning style has no positive impact on his or her learning. But this myth is particularly deeply entrenched in educational circles as discouragingly noted by Rohrer and Pashler (2012): "The contrast between the enormous popularity of the learning-style approach in education and the lack of any credible scientific proof to support its use is both remarkable and *disturbing*" – emphasis mine. But a massive empire of peddlers of this myth and its seeming "oh yeah, I have seen that" allure has led to its persistence. But we, as educators, ought to label this idea as what it actually is: The notion that teaching to a student's preferred learning style helps them learn is a myth; nothing more. There is no reason why you should adapt your lessons for students' so-called preferred learning styles. You might leverage these because they provide a meaningful presentation of a topic in multiple modalities but not because a student prefers them. Content, not preference will determine whether or not a particular approach makes sense and has any real potential to improve learning.

Myth 2: Today's Youth Are Digital Natives

Marc Prensky coined the phrase "digital natives" in which he referred to the generation of young people who have been immersed in technology all their lives. He claimed that they are unique and distinct from all other generations and their unique characteristics include sophisticated technical skills and learning preferences for which traditional approaches cannot deliver. This assertion is, however, utterly false. And worse it is widely propagated by the various businesses and peddlers of so-called *21st century skills* that try to radically transform learning for the digital age.

First off, Presnsky's coining of the term was not based on research into the generation but rather created by rationalizing phenomena that he had observed[1] – in other words, he made it up based on his anecdotal experience. As his idea became popularized many additional claims were added to this initial, made-up, concept. Included among these are the notion that this generation possesses new ways of knowing and being, that they are innately technology savvy, that they are effective multitaskers and collaborators, that they embrace gaming, and that they demand immediate gratification. Each of these additional claims is also, false, excerpt perhaps the last one – but that is not based on any generational trait but based on our allowing them to spend dozens of hours on digital media per week.

While this generation – and likely subsequent ones immersed in such technology-rich environments – do use a large quantity of technologies to communicate, find information, and stay connected with friends while engaging in a digital world they do so for personal empowerment and entertainment, not for learning. In fact, research by Kennedy and Fox (2013) has found that these so-called digital natives are not actually very "digitally literate in using technology to support their learning" (p. 1). They are literate in using the technology only insofar as it helps in their preferred uses – engaging with the digital environment and communicating with their friends. In a large survey of the literature on technology in education, Jones and Shao (2011) note the following:

1. There is no evidence to suggest that terms such as the "net generation" and "digital native" are accurate of the younger generation
2. There is no evidence of a consistent demand from students to change pedagogical styles to embrace claims made associated with those calling for such

In other words, we have no evidence to suggest that this new generation are "digital natives" and furthermore, the evidence I provided in Chapters One and Two about how we learn would still hold even if so. And as a coup de grace against the desire to cultivate multitasking as inherent to what people in the digital age do, research actually suggests that engaging in multitasking is devastating for individuals. Specifically, we find that in multitasking, we unknowingly enter an addiction loop where novelty is rewarded by a shot of dopamine again, and again, which makes us less capable of concentrating[2]. Consequently, education does not need to embrace the digital shift and radically transform itself; rather, it would be prudent to include technology in learning only insofar as it enhances the content and skill being learned. In any case that it does not; there is no reason to use any technology, even for the misnamed "digital natives".

Myth 3: The Learning Pyramid Accurately Describes Best Instructional Practice

Many teachers embrace the "Learning Pyramid" because when we first started teaching, we realized how little we knew and, after teaching, we realized how much more we understood it. This truism many of us have experienced puts up a smokescreen over the reality of what is going on with learning. The actual truth of the matter is that the learning pyramid we hear about commonly in education today is pretty much entirely made up and, consequently, is not worth considering seriously in terms of its relationship to effective instruction for learning. What is this learning pyramid? Let's survey it briefly.

Way back in 1946, Edgar Dale presented his *Cone of Experience* (example image found in Figure 3.1), which is the forerunner to modern manipulations.

That cone is a visual device to classify learning experiences as very concrete (at the bottom) to very abstract (at the top). Texts, for instance, composed of symbols are very abstract whereas direct, purposeful experience is concrete. There is nothing wrong with the cone of experience as far as it was

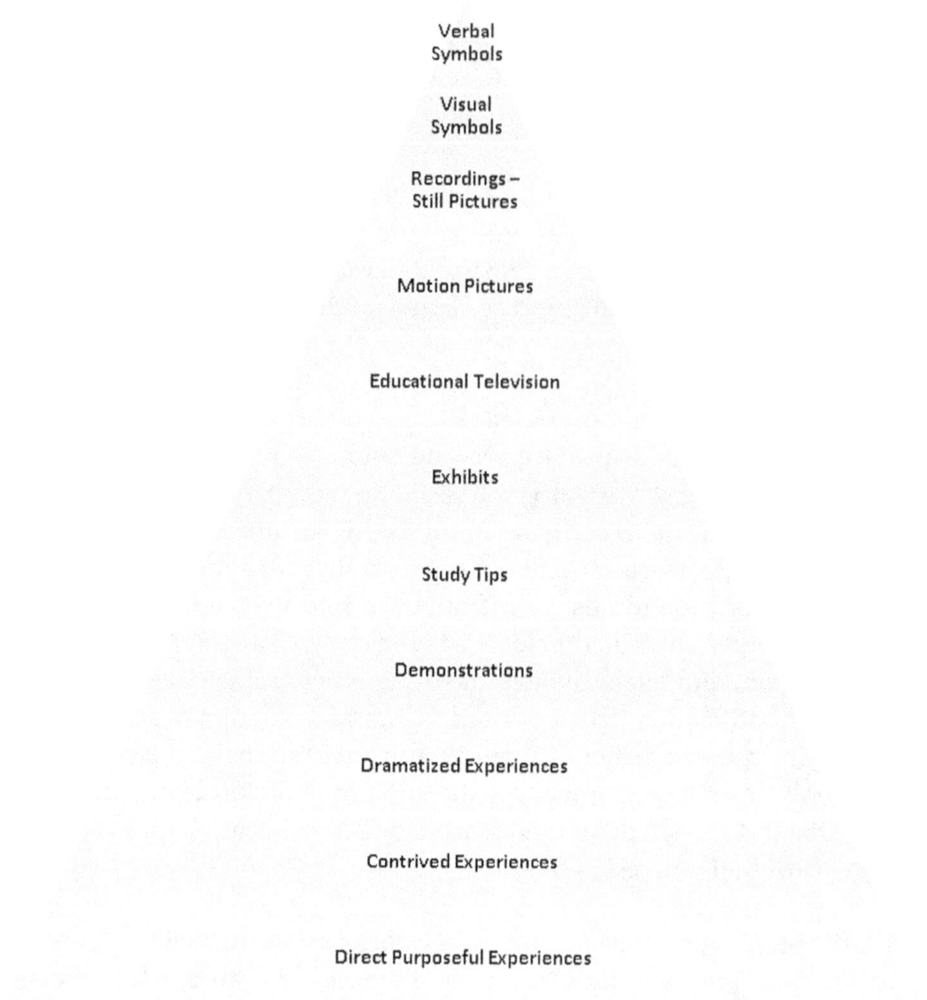

```
                    Verbal
                    Symbols

                    Visual
                    Symbols

                  Recordings –
                  Still Pictures


                 Motion Pictures


              Educational Television


                    Exhibits


                   Study Tips


                 Demonstrations


              Dramatized Experiences


              Contrived Experiences


           Direct Purposeful Experiences
```

Figure 3.1 Dale's original cone of experience.

initially constructed. It simply attempts to delineate among which types of experiences are more and less abstract.

Dale did not use any pedagogical practices in his original cone and, more importantly, there were absolutely no numbers associated with his cone. About the cone, he said: "The cone is a visual metaphor of learning experiences, in which the various types of audio-visual materials are arranged in order of increasing abstractness as one proceeds from direct experience".

Modern educators, very likely based on philosophical predispositions, have manipulated his cone to include pedagogical labels and percentages, none of which is based on any real research. Figure 3.2 includes an example of such a manipulation although I have aptly marked it as false so no

Learning Myths and Other Nonsense ◆ 39

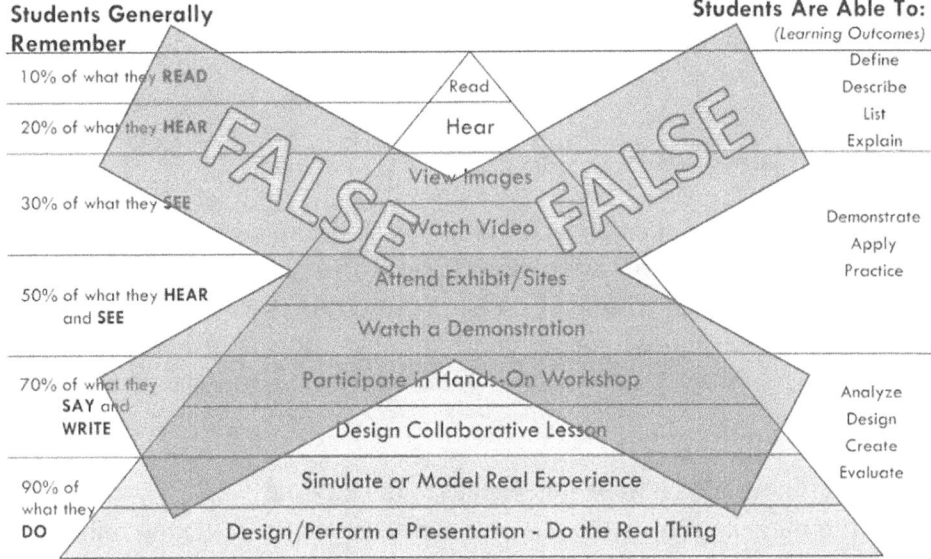

Figure 3.2 Manipulated cone of experience.

one skimming through this gets the wrong idea! Manipulations like this are entirely made up…

Does it matter that it's just made up? You bet it does! Lalley and Miller (2007) provide perhaps the best critique of this perversion of Dale's Cone of Experience and point out the following elements that would have to be considered if this were to be demonstrated as true:

1. The methods would have to be of the same duration to be meaningfully compared
2. The same teacher should carry out the experiment
3. The content to be learned with each method should be the same
4. The outcome measures should actually measure retention/recall after a time delay

Unfortunately, for those who use the Learning Pyramid skewed towards such ends, there is absolutely ZERO research that has shown the perfectly rounded off percentages for these pedagogical practices. So, next time you see this one, cringe, and politely share its faulty basis. It is unfortunately one of the more pervasive myths in education today. And it is undoubtedly something that we should not let convince us of anything with regards to what is considered "best practice".

Having surveyed three widely held myths about learning that we all ought to disavow moving forward let us now turn to some even worse things peddled in educational circles today. Outright nonsense that is shared all too frequently that can be, on its face, shown to be illogical.

Nonsense in Education

Beyond the widespread belief in these myths there is also a great deal of nonsense peddled throughout education. Equally we must confront such nonsense and expose it for what it is – false. Furthermore, we must be willing to act on the fact that these ideas do not hold any water and thus we must be cautious when we see this nonsense peddled by even those with whom we agree.

Nonsense 1: Knowledge Is Irrelevant Thanks to the Internet

One of the more common notions of the past two decades is the notion that knowledge is no longer important because of the Internet. This idea is rotten at its core: It both fails the test of time-tested wisdom (trivium's emphasis on grammar stage) and current empirical research (one of the most established truths about learning is that learning requires knowing things).

First, let's clarify what is typically meant by those who affirm this nonsensical claim (which, they of course, do not believe to be nonsense). A perfect example of this belief is when someone claims: "You don't need to memorize factual information because you can just look it up on the Internet"! So, let's break this down to a list of premises underlying the logic that leads to a conclusion and assess the quality of this claim. As we look at each of the premises I outline below I will take care to present why it is reasonable to assume that a person espousing this nonsensical claim agrees with the premise and reflect on whether or not each premise is more likely true or false.

- Premise 1: Learning requires knowledge of things
- Premise 2: Before the Internet people had to memorize knowledge of things
- Premise 3: Knowledge can be found easily on the Internet
- Conclusion: Therefore, knowledge does not need to be memorized

Premise 1: Learning requires knowledge of things. Within the claim, "you don't need to memorize factual information because you can just look it up on the Internet" we find an implicit acknowledgement that knowledge is necessary for learning. Notice that the point within this statement is that memory is irrelevant not because knowledge does not help but because knowledge is perceived to be readily available. Furthermore, such a claim also affirms that there is benefit to looking those things up. So, I think that we can all agree someone making this claim seems to acknowledge that in order to learn how to create a historical argument, to implement a science experiment, to write an essay (or whatever form of learning) they must leverage and utilize relevant knowledge to do so. And thus, it seems that they agree with the fact that learning requires knowledge of things.

Now, is this premise more likely true or false? The data on this one is strongly in favor of its being true. When it comes to learning, it is what you know that determines what you see and not the other way around[3]. That is to say, your knowledge shapes what you look for, how you filter and connect ideas, how you interpret information, and consequently, knowledge is essential to learning. So, premise #1 seems true.

Premise 2: Before the Internet people had to memorize knowledge of things. Within the claim, "you don't have to memorize factual information *because you can just look it up* on the Internet" we again see an implicit acknowledgement that this *was* true. Notice that there is no denial of the real benefit of knowledge. Such adherents seem to think that because you can "access it" on the Internet now that you don't need to have it readily accessible in your memory.

Now, what about the premise itself; is it more likely to be true or false? It seems fairly obvious that we can all agree this is true. Although there are certainly some people who denigrate the value of memorization, they virtually always point to so-called "rote" memorization. When memorization is referred to as rote it basically means that the person memorizes something but what is memorized is without meaning. This is not the end aim for learning and so it is a reasonable position, but the vast majority of what we memorize is *not rote*. Furthermore, some factual knowledge, memorized through rote processes can help learning by reducing the burden on working memory. And beyond that, virtually the only circumstance in which transfer occurs is when memorized knowledge is applied elsewhere. And this can – and does – occur in cases where one has no "why" or "how" knowledge whatsoever.

For instance, if I ask you to paint a picture in your mind two parallel and vertical lines of equal length connected in the middle by a shorter, perpendicular line you might envision….

- H

You did not need to understand H, or know *why* H, or anything else. Instead, you only needed to memorize "H". Memorized information is crucially important and educators need to stop denigrating it. What we know – which is basically the definition of memorized information – frames what we see and not vice-a-versa. In any case, herein we are specifically showing that virtually everyone agrees that memorization of some things is important for learning.

Clearly, before the Internet existed, people did have to memorize factual knowledge to use it when it was appropriate. The difference between someone who would make the nonsensical claim that memorization no longer matters and wise person is that those who are wise would strike out the first three words of the premise and replace had with have to so it would read: "People have to memorize knowledge of things" because it is still true. Okay, so what about this third premise?

Premise 3: Knowledge can be found easily on the Internet. This one is not so clear-cut. First off, knowledge is not well clarified. Is everything you find on the Internet true? Of course not. Do the search engines skew what you find based on their filters, their designers' algorithms and preferences, and your prior searches? Yes, they do. So, already we are finding that simply searching online is messy in that *anything goes* and there are filters, which you may or may not be actively aware of, that skew what you find. This is particularly problematic in that we have the established understanding that humans tend to confirm what they already believe (called *confirmation bias*). In other words, the filters on which your searches for information are skewed will increasingly mirror what you already believe and delude you into thinking you are correct when, in fact, you may not be. The Internet, Google, Facebook, and other information gatekeepers in today's world make confirmation bias infinitely easier to take hold over our thinking thanks to algorithms designed to give us more of what we like. By catering to each individual, as aided by these algorithms and the cookies stored in our computer, the search engines operate in a way that is downright detrimental for learning in that it enhances the influence of confirmation bias.

Furthermore, a simple search online for knowledge is far more complex than one might imagine. As we have noted earlier, there are a few principles of learning we should bring back up in this context. Of the highest importance: *We should respect cognitive limits*. Recall that our working memory is limited and anything we do not have stored in long-term memory eats up at that limited space. If I do not know that the Election of 1800 symbolized the peaceful transition of one party to another in American history, yes, I can look that up but seeing it gives me the illusion that I know it. In any work that I do with this – which is typically what we want, to go *deeper* – that still eats up at my working memory because I do NOT know it. So, my search is hindered because I am eating up precious space in my working memory on foundational things that I ought to have memorized.

Using any search engine to find information simply deludes you into thinking you can now move deeper. The truth is you have hindered your working memory – your cognitive filter on learning – and your ability to go deeper has been reduced significantly compared to someone who already knows that by having stored it in his or her long-term memory. Finally, this does not even consider the complexity involved in a simple online search for information. Let's think of just a few of the steps involved: (1) You must choose a particular set of relevant search terms, (2) you must filter tens of thousands of results, (3) you must hone in on which are most likely true, and (4) you must then select the "good" source and navigate through it to get the specific information you need requiring you to filter out what is superficial and what is relevant. The problem here is that this conflicts again with multiple principles of learning. The first is the same as mentioned before: *We should respect cognitive limits*. Notice that we are no longer talking about one "piece of information" but I have just listed four distinct things, each of which is burning away at your working memory. But that is not all. This also conflicts with several other principles of learning: *Learning requires thought; breadth of essentials is foundational;* and *learning early and late are significantly different.* When someone searches online for information, they encounter many hyperlinks, advertisements, and so forth, each of which distract our thought from the point at hand to other areas. This hinders our ability to learn. Next, the claim itself implicitly devalues the principle of learning that mastering a broad base of essential knowledge is foundational to successfully going deeper. Finally, this list of four steps are all things that experts can handle, while novices cannot. In other words, the claim that knowledge is irrelevant thanks to the Internet violates more of what we know about how learning works than it fits with. I have only briefly expanded on each of these because hopefully the point is crystal clear – to think that "googling" something is sufficient for learning to occur is nonsense.

What about a tool such as Amazon's *Alexa* or its equivalent? These could be helpful, however, in other ways they could make things worse, actually. These are programmed to complete auto-searches that rely on top hits preferred by the company of whatever product you are using. That means that each of these devices have already been engineered to present, as fact, every topic filtered through a particular vantage point. Alexa has been noted to heavily rely on Wikipedia, to present as factual heavily skewed ideology[4], and, since it's linked to Amazon, it will fill up your cart with things you do not need to buy that are "recommended"!

Surely, educators cannot imagine that allowing a computer to tell you what to think is true is a recipe for deep learning, right?! As humans we ought not to cede our critical thinking over to machines but rather, we ought to cultivate these capacities ourselves so that we are not enslaved to reliance upon them for answering basic and advanced questions. Putting blind faith in the honor and wisdom of Amazon, Google, Facebook, or whatever company to be a gatekeeper and framer of everything you learn is not a great pathway to cultivate fair and independent humans.

The ease of access to information and the seeming power through which search engines provide us to navigate what is available to us lead to the illusion of not needing knowledge. However, it is just an illusion, and in reality, they truly serve as a crutch – if not an outright disease – damaging your ability to learn well as they become necessities that you rely on. Knowledge that you hold in your memory remains, perhaps the paramount ingredient to future learning. Anything you have stored in your memory is *yours – you own it*. You do not need to ask anyone, you don't need to look it up; you don't need some corporation to tell you what you should think of it. Your mind is the most powerful tool for engaging with information in the universe (at least that we know of). The Internet has not changed that. The bottom line here is that the ease of access to information we have is not a recipe for learning, it is a recipe for distraction, deception, and delusion. Unless we take careful, and purposeful steps to counteract these, we will promote an environment that will give more strength to the influence that confirmation bias – and the opinions of powerful companies like Google and Amazon – over our own understanding of the world and that is not a good thing.

Nonsense 2: Truth Is Just a Social Construct

The notion that "truth" is just a social construct has become increasingly widespread over the past few decades. This belief is widely believed in education because of a faulty extension of social constructivist learning theory. This is another topic I have dealt with in more detail elsewhere[5] and I encourage you to look at those for further expansion but herein I want to emphasize the illogical nature of such a view. Put simply, constructivist learning theory suggests that people construct meaning in their own mind and thus, learning is a process that the individual must do. This is perfectly compatible with what I shared in Chapters One and Two and, indeed, is a viable theory for learning. Before we get to the problem, let's expand this to clarify another theory, derived from and related to constructivism: Social constructivism. Basically, this extends constructivism by maintaining that human development is socially situated and that knowledge is constructed through interaction with others – in social settings. As such, it creates the broad view that since we are social creatures, and that each of us creates our own meaning, that this means that the collective understanding is also a product of individuals, and therefore, a "social construct". Again, this is not necessarily a problem nor does it contradict any principle I have noted thus far, so what is the issue?

The problem arises when people make what appears to be a logical extension of this theory and apply it at scale. Since knowledge is constructed in individual's minds *and* knowledge is co-constructed in societies the extension that some people argue is that it means all knowledge is simply our own creation. This pushes a radical subjectivism, which renders all knowledge entirely and hopelessly relative and, in effect, nothing more than opinion. This is a problem because if true, then we can never know true reality and we will always be stuck in our own viewpoint, influenced by those around us, but unable to claim to actually know what is true. In other words, if we adopt this idea our pursuit of truth is over in earnest. If we do claim to pursue truth, we are just agreeing to play a game knowing that it is a lie. In either case, since truth is no longer something independent of us, we seek to change what is "true" so as to meet our own personal and political views. The attempt to objectively pursue an understanding of what is truly real will be replaced with devastating consequences. One path it may lead is a commitment that is political in nature resulting in the use of force to compel others to believe as we do. Another path it may lead to is an entirely practical outlook that focuses only on what matters right now in our exact context and not caring about anything else. Or another possible path it will lead is one that includes a completely self-centered outlook where the only thing that matters is self-fulfillment. Each of these paths draw us into faulty aims for education because we lose the single best one – the steadfast pursuit of truth.

So, having established that this is a problem let us now turn to its illogical line of reasoning. This claim is completely self-contradictory because it fails to meet its own standard. That is, the claim is universal but the claim fits into that reality so it is actually internally incoherent. Let's explain through a series of bullet points as I think that will help us make better sense of this…

- Claim: Truth is just a social construct
- Problem: Is that truth just a social construct?
- Well…
- If yes, then it seems to say we should doubt it because it is not actually true but simply a construction of society and, therefore, of no more value to believe than its negation – or literally anything else for that matter!
- If no, then how is it that this one universal truth can be known outside the others that are mere constructions of society – isn't that incredibly arbitrary?!

Ultimately, this claim cannot live up to its own standard so it is what philosopher's label internally incoherent and therefore, nonsense. Do not let this nonsense gain foothold in the halls of your school except as an exercise in analytic philosophy!

Summary

We should avoid myths such as the claim that teaching to a child's preferred learning style improves their learning. We should avoid myths that today's youth, because they have grown up in a technologically-infused society are somehow "wired" differently in how they learn as so-called digital natives. We should avoid myths such as the claim falsely made that the learning pyramid reflects anything meaningful about how to improve learning. But it is not just myths that we need to avoid. There are also outright lies and nonsense peddled in educational circles that we also need to recognize and challenge. It is absolute nonsense to claim that memorizing factual knowledge has been rendered irrelevant thanks to the Internet. If anything, knowledge is even more important to filter the bombardment of information we encounter in our world of information overload. It is complete nonsense to believe that truth is merely a social construct or a tool used by the powerful to keep their positions of authority. Each of these claims is grounded in completely internally contradictory foundations and are, thus, necessarily false.

There is a great deal of information peddled about education and learning in today's world. It is important that we not discount ideas others hold but that we critically analyze new ideas we encounter to determine whether they are more or less likely to be true. Beyond this, however, there are also many false ideas that have taken hold in education and we need to be aware of them. These false ideas include myths about learning, which are harmless delusions at best, and detrimental to learning at worst. These false ideas also include outright nonsense, which significantly alters our purpose for education in ways that are detrimental to meaningful learning.

For Reflection and Application

Thinking back on this chapter, consider the following reflective tasks and ideas for application in your classroom:

1. Which of the myths have you seen most prominently in education?
2. Are there any of these myths that you allow to influence your practice?

3   How might you make modifications to move away from letting them influence you (or others) productively?
4   Reflect on how you have seen the examples of nonsense in this chapter in education? What can you do to improve students' experience with these ideas?

Notes

1. Kirschner, P.A. & van Merrienboer, J.J.G. (2013). Do learners really know best? Urban legends in education. *Educational Psychology*, 48(3): 1–15.
2. Wolf, M. (2018). *Reader, come home: The reading brain in the digital age.*
3. Paul Kirschner frequently states this and I think it is as brilliant as it is elegant.
4. Examples are plenty, but one illustration of this ideological skew is that of presenting gender is a spectrum as certainly true. However, based on current evidence, this remains a highly contentious claim. This very new idea is not derived from empirical data but rather from presuppositions of Critical Theory applied to society – hence it gives an ideological skew tied to Critical Theory's origins.
5. Krahenbuhl, K.S. (2016). Student-centered education and constructivism: Challenges, concerns, and clarity for teachers. *The clearing house: A journal of educational strategies, issues, and ideas*, 89(3): 97–105.

PART II
FRAMEWORK
How Do We Do This?

4

The Trivium: A Classical Method

There are many aspects that go into a classical approach to education. However, one central component of the classical approach is the *Trivium*. The trivium is not some innovative ploy that has emerged along with the cacophony of other claims from the so-called 21st century skills movement. The trivium is a tried and tested approach to education and I will argue herein that it is an incredibly powerful approach to organizing learning that leads to more enduring and deep knowledge. The Trivium, being a product of the past is for our reference – something from which we ought to learn. And in light of the best current empirical data we have regarding learning there is good reason to hold fast to it and leverage it in our contemporary world and our unique contexts. But we ought not to reside in it alone; but to learn from it and to allow it, as part of the tried and tested wisdom of the past, to inform our future.

Although I am a history educator, I am not going to spend much time on historical development of the classical approach. The reason for this is that its historical development does not have significant bearing on the focus of this book. Instead, I will point you to a free online resource that would be worthy of exploring should you be interested in examining the historical development of classical education[1]. But I will emphasize that what is commonly understood in our world as *classical education* was formalized in the Middle Ages when the curriculum of the *trivium* ("three ways") and *quadrivium* ("four ways") were utilized as the basic framework for education.

The primary focus for classical education in the sense that relates most directly to this book – and to your application of these ideas – is an emphasis on the trivium of *grammar, logic,* and *rhetoric.* The *quadrivium* of the Middle Ages consisted of astronomy, arithmetic, music, and geometry. However, we can imagine these as the specific domains of knowledge[2] worthy of study in a broad and meaningful education. Also, we can concur with influential scholar Hirsch (1988) that in determining what is essential for one's liberal education we need to examine a society's cultural literacy.

Ultimately, because of this, throughout the book I be placing emphasis on the trivium and the modified use of it as the central piece to a framework for learning in any context. This is because the three stages of grammar, logic, and rhetoric are extremely malleable and, once understood, they truly serve as tools for learning that both teacher and student alike can master and have an intelligent plan to learn and succeed in *any* domain. I would argue that the curriculum beyond that (the quadrivium, if you will) should be solidly grounded in the liberal arts tradition and I will offer an expansion of what this might look like in later chapters.

The Trivium: An Overview

At its most fundamental level, the goal of learning through the trivium is to equip students with the tools that they will need to learn on their own. In this way, learning through the trivium is a liberating mindset that leads to the emergence of a pattern for learning that empowers the learner. This is, in fact, why the use of the trivium is so common within those who advocate for a liberal education – it is to *liberate* the learner to be equipped for learning on his or her own. First, this approach recognizes that development of a broad and sufficient foundation of essential knowledge to engage is the starting point for learning. Second, after having established a broad foundation, they begin to build upon it through logical analysis by asking challenging questions that sharpen understanding and require extended precision and clarification. And third, they apply rhetorical tools to articulate their understanding, elegantly, and persuasively, and perhaps most importantly, through a slow process of committing to knowledge building before pontification. In this way, the learners come to recognize a consistent pattern – or form – to their learning. And the three stages of the trivium equip them to see the deep structure of learning so that they develop fundamental tactics and skills for learning any domain sufficiently to engage in it.

Historically, the trivium has been argued to fit naturally with human developmental tendencies and I see no major problem with this claim but urge readers to recognize this is true more broadly rather than aligned to ages and stages. Dorothy Sayers (1948), in an otherwise wonderful article, popularized the notion that these stages ought to be understood as directly tied to physical stages of growth. In particular, she describes each stage in physical development terms: The Poll-parrot, the Pert, and the Poetic. She admits that she is not enlightened about child psychology in the piece and, although her views fit with what people historically imagined as a *natural* development of cognition, they have been discredited over the past half century. This is why I would suggest these are fine to be aware of but not to live and die on – they are not, in and of themselves, the trivium. The age stages imagined by many are a faithful reflection on the trivium, which is more or less experientially true, albeit not absolutely true.

In her description[3], the Poll-parrot stage is one in which the child "readily memorizes the shapes and appearances of things" and "likes to recite", "rejoices in chanting of rhymes", and so on. She explains that in the Pert stage is "characterized by contradicting, answering-back, liking to "catch people out" (especially one's elders), and the propounding of conundrums". She classifies the final stage as the Poetic Age, which is "self-centered", "yearns to express itself", "rather specialises in being misunderstood", and is "restless and tries to achieve independence". Table 4.1 outlines the trivium's three stages below and a collection of when each stage applies, what is the focus

Table 4.1 Trivium Stages Across Cognitive Development

	Stage I: Grammar ⇨	Stage II: Logic ⇨	Stage III: Rhetoric
When	Early cognitive development in a domain	Mid cognitive development in a domain	Later cognitive development in a domain
What	• Fundamental facts of a domain • Language, Grammar, Syntax, Structure, Vocabulary	• Rules of Logic • Principles and Relations • Comparison and Contrast • Questioning • Evaluation	• Articulate Communication • Application • Synthesis • Creative Expression
How	Reading; Singing/Chanting; Repetition	Reading; Discussion; Debate; Practice; Evaluation	Reading; Discussion; Speeches; Practice; Creation
Why	Equip with *foundations*, clarity of domain's broad scope, description, and narrative	Equip with *tools of reasoning*, assessment of thought, and skill in accurate comparison/contrast	Equip with skills for *articulate* persuasion, precision and *creative expression*

for learning, strategies for how to help succeed in each stage, and a rationale for the why of each stage.

While Sayers' characterizations do fit our experience of the natural development of children, we should remember to be cautious about drawing inferences that these are (a) natural or (b) tied to any physical development within the trivium. Insofar as the trivium is a focus in this book I want to make it explicit that *the progressions through these stages should be understood as being compatible with cognitive development; not physical development*. The "how" elements of Table 4.1 are derived for considering the trivium in a typical K-12 setting and thus do fit with Sayers' conceptions but they are malleable and could easily be modified depending on the learner's particular context.

Take for instance, if I, an adult of 38 years of age at the time of this writing, were to decide to learn an entirely new discipline – let's say theoretical physics. Applying this framework, I would begin at the grammar stage and focus on memorization of the fundamental facts of that domain. As I am older, chanting and rhyming may not be something that is particularly appealing to me as they are to young children but I would be foolish to not leverage the benefits of memorization strategies. I might simply recite, rather like those in Christian churches recite the Apostle's Creed, to memorize the basic essential aspects of belief. As I grew in understanding (remembering the essential knowledge of theoretical physics) I would move into the logic stage. At this point, while I would not be an emerging teenager always asking why and challenging my elders, I would be wise to start to engage critically with the ideas of the domain. And applying the fundamental laws of logic to that domain is an incredibly powerful means through which to ask tough questions and dive deep into the domain. Finally, as I reached more advanced stages of learning I would reach the rhetoric stage and again, while I would not be at the age of adolescence with an emerging desire to classify my own identity, I would draw upon the goals of articulately expressing views about the domain. This is a short sample to illustrate a larger point: These stages are not directly tied to physical development; they are linked directly to cognitive development. As such, any learner, at any age, should consider applying these stages to their learning and modify the "how" aspects of the stage while keeping the purposes of each.

So, Table 4.1 outlines some general patterns across the trivium of the classical model, which provide a systematic engagement for the learner as an active member of the great conversations of mankind. As such, it is important that we not confuse these stages as being associated solely with physical development. Insofar as we are interested in the stages it is primarily due to their benefits for each subsequent stage of cognitive development. In summary, early on in a learner's understanding in any domain there should be much more direct instruction where the expert in the room (the teacher and quality books) guides the student intentionally to understand the essentials. As a learner becomes more competent in a domain there can be a meaningful transition towards more student-led learning because this pattern for learning is intentional in training the mind in the art of learning fostering tools for self-learning in the future as the learner knows the pattern to apply.

Stage I: Grammar
The trivium originated through reflection on the norms of experience for children as they develop cognitively. Any adult who interacts on a consistent basis with youth will acknowledge that at an early age they love repetition. Parents, do you remember when your children asked for the same book to be read again, and again, *and again…?* Or do you recall when they would ask you to play the same game over and over *and over*? Young children sing to themselves; they repeat their favorite parts of stories and movies over and over while they play, and because of their reasonable ignorance[4] about the world are naturally curious to learn as much as they can about it.

Young children, then, seem naturally predisposed to prefer repetition. Consequently, the classical approach leverages this seemingly innate characteristic to build up a rich and broad foundation of basic factual knowledge. While the general patterns of younger students somewhat naturally tending towards repetition as a benefit for enhancing learning this stage would hold true as the initiation for learning in any domain and at any age. So, while later in life we may not (at least I don't!) have this inclination towards singing and continual repetition it is a helpful practice to recognize as important the use of memorization strategies to successfully complete this first foundational stage.

This is referred to as the *grammar* stage. Young learners are taught the basic foundations for communication in the domain. Just as grammar is the foundation for language this stage is focused primarily on providing the foundational knowledge-base necessary to engage in deeper thinking in a particular domain. This does, of course, include actual grammar and phonics but the choice of the phrase, "Grammar stage" is more a classification for any domain. The grammar stage is focused on building knowledge of the key ideas, patterns, and rules in a domain so that they can build off that foundational knowledge-base.

At its very heart, the grammar stage is about understanding important information in a domain at an introductory level. We are not focused on deep mastery understanding but a generally broad range of essential material stored in the students' long-term memory. Getting the essential knowledge into our long-term memory is, then, the heart of our first stage of learning.

Stage II: Logic

As the learner grows and starts to challenge every adult request and ask questions about why this and why that in a more interrogative way than when they are younger this tendency, too, is leveraged. Of course, young children will ask why about pretty much everything but that is the genuine curious sense. Here we are referring to that point at which the adolescent learner is inclined to *challenge* with why; not just ask to satisfy his thirst for knowing. In this second phase of learning, classical education places emphasis on leveraging that predisposition towards disagreement and brings in nuance. So, this stage generally ought to include the teaching of *logic* providing a framework from which they can think critically and coherently. However, again, this is also applicable to the learning of a new domain.

The *logic stage* in that way would place emphasis on requiring comparison and contrast of divergent perspectives. This phase would prioritize representing opposing views accurately and evaluating them. It would include careful consideration of the implications of different understandings, and so forth. In this manner, the focus now looks less at knowledge of basic facts as primary aim and instead placing emphasis on exploring cause and effect; on comparison and contrast; on effective and ineffective argument; and so on.

At the foundation of all reasoning rest so-called *first principles*. These are foundational, self-evident statements that underlie everything else we reason with. There include three traditional first principles – commonly referred to as the laws of logic. First, the Law of Noncontradiction, which simply says that something cannot be both "x" and "not x" in the same time and context. For example, I am either typing the words you are reading right now or I am not – I cannot both by typing and not typing at the same time and in the same context – that would require some qualification. There are no exceptions to this rule. The Islamic medieval theologian, Avicenna, had a funny way of challenging those who wished to deny the law of noncontradiction. He wrote that anyone who denies the law of noncontradiction should be beaten and burned until he admits that to be beaten is not the same as not to beaten, and to be burned is not the same as not to be burned[5]! Perhaps over the top but his illustration is a helpful one – there is no way around this law; it's at work in all our reasoning, all the time. This law is the primary and most important law of logic.

The second law of logic is the law of the excluded middle, which basically states that something either is or is not. It excludes the possibility of something being both existing and not existing and as such operates very similarly to the law of non-contradiction. The third law of logic is the law of identity, which simply states that something is what it is. When I say that I am typing on a laptop computer you know, broadly, what is being referred to. I am not using a typewriter, not handwriting, nor even using an iPad, for instance. You know what a laptop computer is even if you do not know which brand, and so forth. This is crucial because words must have shared meaning that people agree to, for if they do not, meaningful reasoning is not possible. And the use of logic is really about asking questions, assembling evidence, and using reason to guide us closer to what is true.

Coming to understand these laws of logic guides interaction with the many questions each of us has about the world around us. They provide us a healthy, consistent set of rules that guide all reasoning. And this is a central point of the logic stage – to understand the rules and patterns that govern a domain. In this case, reasoning is broader than most of our classroom subjects and so it might be wise to help your learners become familiar with these through your context because they are at work in what they do in your history, or science, or math class, and so forth.

There is a great deal more to logic but this basic primer should serve to give you an understanding of how it helps move learning forward. As the learner comes to understand that the process of learning requires asking questions, continually refining and sharpening understanding, and cultivating a more nuanced recognition of the various perspectives on the subject-matter he or she will grow in their depth of learning and be ready to move forwards to expressing him or herself.

Stage III: Rhetoric

At the latter stages of learning, the learner again seems to be naturally drawn towards expressing themselves with passion and persuasion. In this phase, classical education teaches students *rhetoric* so that they are not just vocal agents about whatever is on their mind but rather are elegant and persuasive speakers. Furthermore, because they have moved intentionally through these stages, they have a broad foundation of knowledge and training in sound reasoning so they are equipped to be much more eloquent, nuanced, and wise in terms of articulating their own views. In fact, using the framework of the trivium is a wonderful approach to avoid allowing students to violate the wisdom of Aristotle when he said: "The wise man speaks when he has something to say; the fool speaks because he has to say something". As youth grow up, the less broad their knowledge-base, the less accurate they understand views outside of their own narrow opinions, the more they tend towards foolish spouting off of their ignorance. So, the trivium's three stages would be a cogent fortress against such sloppy reasoning and irrelevant pontification, which would result in great benefits for society at large[6].

So, in this brief overview of the trivium I have presented both the trivium framework as a method for learning generally and a model to adapt into each domain. It is in this way that the trivium achieves its dual purposes of: (1) Developing broad and sufficient knowledge to engage in the society in which they are entering *and* (2); learning fundamental tactics and skills for learning any domain sufficiently to engage in it. A learner exposed to this framework over both macro (K-12 course sequence; College program curriculum – domains; etc.) and micro levels (Courses, Units of Learning, etc.) of their educational experience will successfully attain both and be well equipped for succeeding in any endeavor they pursue in life.

Other Important Elements of a Classical Education

Among the most important features of a classical education that moves beyond the bounds of the trivium is that the curriculum itself is coherent. That is, all learning ought to be interrelated. Traditionally, this was affirmed on the basis that all knowledge was acknowledged to be "God's knowledge" that humanity was blessed with uncovering. Because God is acknowledged as a rational and coherent agent, the knowledge should also fit neatly into a unified pattern. In fact, it is mankind's long-standing effort to find unity amongst the diversity around us that led to the origin – and name – of the university. Personally, I believe that this is correct and is, consequently, the best-case scenario for developing a coherent curriculum. However, in the public-school system such an approach is likely to be viewed as inappropriate since it invokes God (not any one religion, albeit) so I will place emphasis on the importance for curricula to be coherent and considered in light of connections within and across domains. In whatever setting you find yourself, it is important to consider how the interlocking domains of knowledge *connect* with one another. This is not necessarily because there is meaningful transfer across them but rather that the more we help learners weave their understanding of disciplines to one another, the stronger their connections will be, and that is a good thing for learning.

In *Wisdom and Eloquence*, Robert Littlejohn and Charles T. Evans argue well for the use the trivium as a means for developing two traits. Within their piece, they explain that for the classical educator the first essential component of learning is remembering. They go on to say that the essence of effective teaching is helping learners, at all stages, to remember critical content and skills and how to apply them. The necessary second component of learning is described as thinking – suggesting that thinking about something extends beyond simply remembering it. This parallels very well with the evidence

I have synthesized with regards to learning in Chapters One and Two. And that is where we will shift to next – clearly presenting the overlap between the trivium, as derived from classical education, and contemporary evidence from cognitive science.

So, recapping then, the classical method is, in its essence, a pattern for learning. It was formalized in response to what seemed to be natural tendencies in our development with regards to learning. However, and perhaps more interestingly, it has gained credence from empirical data published over the past several decades in cognitive science. Using this link between pattern for learning and the research (evidence) from cognitive science what we are led to is the fact that this approach is actually a wonderful system for organizing content/skills in *any domain of learning*[7]. Let us first present an exploration of the alignment and areas of limited alignment between cognitive research and classical education. From there we can synthesize the ideas into a system from which we can constitute our own learning environments and enhance learning.

Alignment of Old and New

In this section I want to walk through the three stages of the trivium and explore how each is supported by the preponderance of the best empirical evidence currently available. But first and foremost, let us take a step back to a macro-level view and think about the big picture. One of the most effective ways to help learners according to John Hattie's[8] systematic review of studies on learning was through incorporation of meta-cognitive strategies. These basically focus on thinking about thinking. This is, in fact, exactly what was criticized of the public school system in Dorothy Sayers' oft-quoted piece on *The Lost Tools of Learning:*

> Has it ever struck you as odd, or unfortunate, that to-day, when the proportion of literacy throughout Western Europe is higher than it has ever been, people should have become susceptible to the influence of advertisement and mass-propaganda to an extent hitherto unheard-of and unimagined?… Is it not the great defect of our education to-day [sic] that although we often succeed in teaching our pupil's "subjects", we fail lamentably on the whole in teaching them how to think? They learn everything, except the art of learning.[9]

At the core of the trivium framework is emphasis on thinking about thinking. The point is to help the learner not only achieve at learning the particular subject (or domain) but to recognize that learning, while not purely linear, does successfully occur through a particular sequence. And the trivium's sequence of grammar in which one builds factual knowledge as a foundation, to the logic stage that engages them in evaluating the claims and assertions made, through the rhetoric stage of constructing informed opinion the learners are engaged in a systematic meta-cognitive endeavor. So, before moving through each stage it is helpful to note that the overall framework provides learners with not just tools for learning beyond what is learnt in the classroom but also equips them with meta-cognitive capacity building throughout. With that said, let's move through the three stages and illustrate the alignment of each with the best evidence on learning that we currently have.

One of the strongest sources of evidence from cognitive science comes from *retrieval practice*. This is pretty straight-forward but, in effect, it means we focus on pulling information *out* from the learner's mind. That is, they are required to retrieve it from memory – not a phone or other device. One of the single best methods for accomplishing this is through small-stakes quizzes (particularly those that are open questions (no provided answers) and yet with a single answer). This aligns perfectly with the trivium's demand in the grammar stage to ensure the learner is equipped with a body of knowledge. How might this be accomplished? It could be achieved fairly easily through memory tests, show-me boards, short response items, recitations, chants, and so forth. Each of these methods (and there could be countless others) is designed in such a way that it specifically requires the learner to retrieve, or call out the information to mind, which helps protect against forgetting such information. This is a powerful tool for improving learning and one that is embedded directly into the early stages of the trivium by design.

So, we see that the trivium fits quite nicely with contemporary advances in the science of learning, which provide empirical support for practices, methods, and priorities of the trivium. But is it that clear-cut? Why isn't everyone doing this? Before moving forward let us take a moment to interact with some of the challenges that will no doubt be encountered by some in education with regards to taking the framework of the trivium into your classroom.

Considering Challenges

We have undoubtedly seen that there is a great deal of overlap between cognitive science and this trivium-focused approach. But are there areas in which the trivium approach seems to be challenged in light of cognitive science?

The most common area where you will find a challenge is derived to something I have already noted as an incorrect inference. This is the way in which the trivium is widely remarked that its stages are to be associated with ages and similar calls that this is the way we *naturally learn*. It is no doubt you have heard appeals to *natural ways of learning* from all sorts of groups. This is probably because our society seems to be drawn by some appeal to get things that are classified as *natural* – natural ways of healing, the semi-dogmatic commitment some have in organic foods, and so forth. Our contemporary culture seems to have come to believe that natural is somehow better than manufactured. Such a view is silly on its face, after all poison ivy is quite natural and not something that I think most would classify as "good". But when it comes to learning this is another area in which we should be wary of such claims about natural development or physical ages and what is called "developmentally appropriate". This is, what seems to be at the heart of the claims made by those who try to turn the trivium into a description for natural development of the child. This view has further been widely popularized by the influential words of Dorothy Sayers who was quoted earlier. However, this is an incorrect inference[10].

Cognitive science has led to an important distinction about determining what is "appropriate" for learners. In particular, in the vast majority of typical educational cases we should not worry about what is developmentally appropriate in consideration of one's age – or physical development. What we should care about is their relative "cognitive development" in terms of determining what is appropriate. This is determined, in large part, to factors underscored earlier when we examined essential principles of learning. You can, largely, determine what is appropriate for a learner based upon the breadth and depth of relevant knowledge they have at hand to engage in a particular task. Now, this does not mean that physical development has no impact – clearly, if, physically, one is incapable of completing a task then that is important. But this book is focused on learning and learning in terms of what we are primarily interested in, in the context of schooling, is related to cognitive areas, not physical ones.

A second challenge to consider stems from the classical view that all knowledge is interrelated. This is derived primarily from an assumption (a logical one) that since God is coherent, His knowledge would be coherently constructed, and consequently fit neatly. The challenge that results here is when advocates for the Trivium specifically, or classical education generally, make the claim that this means certain skills are transcendent. This is a common claim in progressive education, too, the appeal of *critical thinking* or *creativity* as generic skills that can be cultivated to transcend any domain of learning is appealing. And perhaps there is something to it but the preponderance of evidence at this point suggests something else. In particular, there is very strong empirical evidence, collected across decades that point to the fact that most skills we think of are not general but are actually, *domain specific*. That is, critical thinking is not some generic skill that can be taught devoid of content and then the learner can apply it in all settings. Critical thinking is actually tied to specific practices relevant to each domain that should be taught and expected to be applied within the domain but not perhaps, beyond it.

Again, this seems to me not to be a contradiction of science and classical learning but rather a leap too far. Assuming that all knowledge is interrelated does not preclude the fact that skills may be bound to a particular domain whatsoever. Mathematics and science do overlap; history and science also overlap, but does their overlapping mean that a historical thinking skill such having empathy for historical characters in their historical context and not imposing current values on them so as to contextualize our understanding must necessarily be linked to other domains? No, it does not. So, the fact that certain skills we want to cultivate may be better taught within each unique domain does nothing to the fact that the knowledge is interrelated. And furthermore, just thinking about the principles of learning earlier, we have good evidence to support the building of such connections because it helps to further entrench learning in our webs of understanding thereby making it stronger and easier to access and utilize. So, while this is another area where some apparent distinctions may arise I think, more than anything, it should provide us with a caution in blanket statements about ideas that transcend domains.

Outside of these two areas there are no significant contradictions with the outline of the trivium and the evidence from cognitive science about what leads to improved learning. So, while implementing the 21st century Trivium framework, there is good news and bad news. The good news is simply based on the synthesis of research on learning and its alignment to the Trivium we should not expect any major claims to significantly overhaul it. However, the bad news is that we must be vigilant that we do not read into the trivium that which is not coded into it, such as the dubious claim of "natural" progressions. And that is exactly where we are headed next – how do we engage with new ideas to remain vigilant in our effort to build effective learning environments?

Summary

Within this chapter we have surveyed the trivium including some distinctions of its development as well as a consideration of looking at it as a process for learning. The aim here is to provide a foundation of the why behind this sequence so that when we understand the systematic approach of the stages of grammar, logic, and rhetoric. Having explored this we recapped the alignment of this classic ideal with the best current evidence from cognitive science and also considered some challenges that we ought to interact with. Overall, the trivium offers us a great tool to draw upon, distilled through the wisdom of the ages, to apply the best current evidence we have through. But before we put the pieces together in a systematic framework integrating all of these components let us pause and consider how ought we interact with new claims and evidence?

For Reflection and Application

Thinking back on this chapter, consider the following reflective tasks and ideas for application in your classroom:

1. Thinking about the stages of the trivium, create a quick chart that outlines specific content and skills that would fit into each stage of grammar, logic, and rhetoric.
2. Considering the sequence of the next unit you are teaching, how might you revise that sequence in light of the trivium?

Reflect on the three stages of the trivium I have presented as well as the six principles of learning laid out in Chapters One and Two. How do these reinforce one another? Create your own explanation that describes how the principles align with the trivium.

Notes

1. Online you can check out this wonderful overview of Classical Education by Dr. Christopher Perrin of Classical Academic Press. Within it you will find a section dedicated specifically to historical development: http://classicalsubjects.com/resources/ICE.pdf.
2. If you do study classical education more broadly you will find that there are many nuances to this and I fully acknowledge them. For the sake of simplicity and our purposes here, I will consider them similar to domains or disciplines of knowledge.
3. These can be read in their entirety by downloading the freely available PDF of this online at: https://www.pccs.org/wp-content/uploads/2016/06/LostToolsOfLearning-DorothySayers.pdf. The quotes used here are derived from pages 10 and 11 on that PDF.

4. I use this phrase because they are, in fact, ignorant about the world because of their lack of knowledge and experience. It is, thus, very reasonable that they are ignorant about it so this should not be interpreted as demeaning; it is a statement of fact. And I think we should hold much higher standards for the intellectual capacity of youth than we often do but insofar as the point is here, it is their lack of knowing that often prods them to ask, "why"?
5. Avicenna, *Metaphysics* 1, commenting on Aristotle Topics 1.11.105a4–5.
6. I might suggest that this is even more important in our day-in-age in which time, not accuracy, is what most people feel compelled to respond to – we must speak now lest we look like we don't know! Such an approach is almost certainly a factor in much civil disagreement; if we would take the slow approach we'd be much better off.
7. By domain I am referring to a discipline or a subject (History, Geometry, Physics, e.g.). While we want learners to see the connections across domains, one of the most helpful findings of empirical research in expertise is that skills often do not transfer from one domain to another and so applying the trivium model to each domain makes wonderful sense to address this.
8. Hattie, J. (2009). Visible *learning: A synthesis of over 800 meta-analyses relating to achievement.* New York, NY: Routledge.
9. Full essay available online at: https://classicalchristian.org/the-lost-tools-of-learning-dorothy-sayers/
10. It is useful to note that Mrs. Sayers spoke about this decades before empirical data would challenge her claim so this is not a criticism of her. Considered in the context of her times, what was believed then, and what science has since unfolded she was ahead of her contemporaries. But this is one aspect that we can largely ignore moving forward.

5

Engaging with New Ideas and Evidence

Nearly a century ago, T.S. Eliot wrote that there never was a time when the reading public was so helplessly exposed to the influences of its own time. He went on to note that those who read at all, read so many more books by living authors than by dead authors that it created a completely parochial time, shut off from the past[1]. His criticism undoubtedly holds true in our day. By immersing ourselves so fully in the present moment, we lose sight of the fact that the work of today rests upon generations of living from which wisdom has been filtered. We cannot lose sight of the benefits of the wisdom of the past. But, equally, we need to always weigh our actions based upon the preponderance of the evidence and that entails a serious examination of what the most current, high quality evidence points us towards. Linking those two together is how the 21st Century Trivium was constructed. So, what is this alignment and how do we go about adjusting into the future?

In part one, we surveyed a synthesis of current research with regards to how we learn. We then took a short excursus to examine common myths and nonsense to be aware of. Then, in Chapter four, I outlined the basic framework of the Classical Model for learning and juxtaposed these two fields to achieve two ends: (1) Provide a rationale to my claim that this approach is warranted and (2) to extend and enhance the Classical Model in light of developments in cognitive research on learning. What I have presented thus far is not the *final* word on education, however, if applied correctly, it will prepare you and your learners for the future through respect for the past.

I hope to have conveyed a sense of optimism for educational research thus far because areas within it have uncovered significant developments that enrich our understanding of learning. However, there is plenty of bad research out there (just think of the synthesis of best practice that was satirized in the Introduction). And we must recognize that science is not static – it is dynamic, it builds upon theory and modifies theory in light of newer analyses that consider newer, and often better, information. So, as we move forward, we are going to need to be ready to flex and adapt our current understanding in light of new, high quality, evidence. In the rest of this chapter, I will introduce 5 steps to help you **S.E.A.R.CH** to come to evidence-informed decisions about how to respond to those who say: "The research says".

Engaging with New Ideas Going Forward

Keeping up with new research is easier said than done. First off, there is plenty of bad research out there. And furthermore, educators are often fed downright misinformation, too, as popularizers rush to get things out without fully understanding them, they misinterpret their claims, they draw unwarranted conclusions, spin results or base arguments off poor studies, and so forth. In addition to issues with regards to the quality of research and the accuracy of its representations and interpretations, there is another significant factor to consider and be wary of. That is, *you*. Every individual is predisposed to believe things that we already believe. This is called *confirmation bias*. And it is at work in each of us as we attempt to make sense of the world around us. Consequently, we need to be aware of our own presuppositions. Even when we recognize outcomes – or evidence – that falsifies our understanding, we often apply ad hoc reasoning to explain it away in light of our prior belief. In other words, we tend to find ways to maintain what we already believed by making special-case adjustments.

Even with all these problems, we would be fools to stick our heads in the sand and think we already know all we need to. This book is a powerful tool in your handbook for promoting effective learning for your student(s). But I am optimistic that we will continue to get better so long as we continue to critically examine new research and filter its findings to continually refine our understanding. Secondly, being open to investigating new claims and focusing critically on evidence helps you in your movement towards expertise. On that track, it becomes more probable that you may be able to overcome confirmation bias. So, to help you out in engaging with new ideas going forward, this chapter offers simplified plan of attack.

Let's begin very broadly and then provide a roadmap for you to critically examine future research or claims from others related to learning. So, what exactly is good science? Science is a process that seeks to systematically explain features of the natural world[2]. Science is, then, a cyclical process in the pursuit of truth. As such, the prevailing theory at any given time is viewed by scientists as provisional. Science is self-correcting. That is, it is essential to the scientific process that theories be open and subject to criticism. Science is also cumulative in that new theories emerge to replace old ones but only do so insofar as they better account for what the old theory affirmed *and* provide new insight. Science, at its most basic framework basically involves three interlocking and repeating steps: Observe, theorize, and test, which are displayed in Figure 5.1.

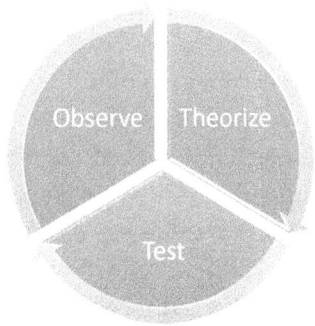

Figure 5.1 The science cycle.

Observation is where the process begins when we collect and measure data to guide the development of a theory to explain what we have found and then we design tests to continually refine our understanding. In this way, we find helpful advice from Sherlock Holmes who would say, "It is a capital mistake to theorize before one has data. Insensibly, one begins to twist facts to suit theories, instead of theories to suit facts[3]". This is a helpful thing to consider as we engage in understanding social sciences – including learning – since it will help keep our theories derived from data and analysis rather than our imagination.

A good tip to remember that is related to this is that if you ever encounter a researcher, ask them if they have ever had to change their mind on anything they are studying. If they cannot give you a specific example of a time when they used to think "x" but now think "y", I would be wary of their skill as a scientist. Given the design of science in our contemporary world as revolving around falsification most science that is serious involves failure and reconsidering what was previously understood. As new observation tools are developed, as new evidence is discovered, as others attempt to replicate findings, the overall experience of science tends towards significant percentages of predictions that turn out to be falsified. So, this short introduction provides a good working outline of what good science is and is summarized in Table 5.1.

Table 5.1 Characteristics of Good Science

Characteristic
Is a process that seeks to measure, understand, and explain the natural world
Is cyclical in the pursuit of truth
Is Dynamic
Is Public and Self-Correcting
Is Cumulative

Beware of Fallacious Reasoning

There are also many things that masquerade as "science" that we ought to be aware of. In particular, these tend to fall into the category of various logical fallacies. We'll only scratch the surface on a few of these, but they are important to helping you interact with new ideas as they often distract us and/or look like evidence even though they are not.

The first fallacy we will look at is called the *ad hominem fallacy*. This comes from the Latin meaning "to the body" and occurs when someone attacks the person presenting a claim rather than the claim itself. A perfect illustration of this is frequently seen in politics when one side name calls the other – "Joe A. Candidate is a Nazi or a Communist!" Since we don't like Nazis nor Communists as they are responsible for millions of deaths, this seems concerning. However, the accusation is just an attack on the person and that may have nothing to do with what they are saying. It is helpful to remember that ideas are not the same as the person who has them and, as such, we need to be aware of ad hominem attacks and move them to where they belong – not as evidence. A second fallacy we'll look at is *the strawman fallacy*. This is also referred to as a caricature. A strawman argument occurs when one person misrepresents another's position by turning it into a simpler and weaker position to attack. An example of this that we commonly see in education is when someone says something like, "Direct Instruction is basically just a blind lecture!" Such a position is easy to attack because no one defends a blind lecture that is completely inattentive to the students. However, this is not direct instruction whatsoever. It is a complete misrepresentation and should be ignored.

The next fallacy we will look at is what is called *equivocation*. This occurs when a word is used with various meanings in a way that is misleading. This has become very common in today's world with the rise of Critical Race Theory (CRT) because of its intentional effort to redefine words as part of their program to change society. CRT assumes that race is all-encompassing, embedded into everything that happens, and that there is always a fight for racial power in all settings. And so, they use words we commonly understand in ways that are not agreed upon[4]. Traditionally, everyone understands that a person is "racist" if he or she is prejudiced against persons of another race, simply on the basis of their race. Everyone agrees that racism is a heinous thing. But CRT assumes that being "not racist" is not possible for white persons. But when a CRT advocate says that someone is a racist, they do not mean that the person is actually racist in the traditional sense, rather, they mean that a white person, by virtue of being white, is in power, privileged, and therefore racist. This causes significant confusion in conversation because these two definitions are contradictory and so unless you qualify each of them, the conversation gets lost in which definition is being assumed in each moment. Furthermore, this specific redefinition of terms is an illustration of reasoning in a circle with their conclusion baked into the definition through their assumptions, which is another fallacy of reasoning called *begging the question*. All of this is not evidence; they simply illustrate fallacious lines of reasoning.

Finally, let's consider one last common fallacy – a *red herring fallacy*. A red herring is a dried fish that smells, but in this context, it is when an irrelevant topic is introduced to divert attention away from the actual topic. An example of this could be at a parent-teacher meeting with the topic of student's poor behavior in mistreatment of his classmates. In the meeting, the parent mentions that she has just switched jobs so their schedules have changed. While that may be true, the parent's job and the schedule at home does not have any direct bearing on the child's behavior towards other students in the classroom – it is a red herring that distracts us from what is being discussed. So, we've just examined only four fallacies of reasoning and I encourage you to study more of these as they are commonly found and distract us from real evidence[5].

Acknowledge Cognitive Biases

Beyond fallacious reasoning, we also have to deal with our own cognitive biases. These are things that are hard-wired into how our minds interact with the world and cannot be simply "turned off". However, awareness of them can help us reduce their influence on how we interact with new information. Although psychological research has found a great number of these, I am going to examine just a small set of biases that are particularly relevant for our context.

We already looked at one of these earlier – *confirmation bias*. If you recall, this is simply a predisposition to confirm things that we already believe and it influences what questions we ask, how we interpret vague information, and so forth. The other biases operate similarly. *Anchoring bias* is a tendency to over-rely on the first piece of information we encounter when learning in a new domain. *Recency bias* refers to the fact that we tend to weigh the latest information that we encounter more heavily than older data – often without the new information being of more value. Another bias we all have to deal with is *bandwagon bias*, or the tendency to fall into groupthink. Often, we tell ourselves – without saying anything – that since others I know believe this, I believe this, too. Humans, however, have a long history of getting things wrong, so don't get swept up solely because of the prevailing opinion of the day. The last of these cognitive biases I will note here is *availability bias* where we tend to overestimate the importance of information that is available. Each of these biases are simply hardwired into how we think and as a result, we will want to reflect on them periodically to ask ourselves: Is one of these biases potentially skewing how strongly I stand on this topic?

The S.E.A.R.CH Process

Having outlined what good science is, what it is not, and pointing out some common fallacies and biases to be aware of, now we will shift into how we can critically examine research and/or claims people make. Recall that the scientific process is cyclical and consists at the most basic level of three steps: Observation, theorizing, and testing. These are important to recall because when looking at research critically, each of these steps can be checked for quality. So, here is a five-step roadmap to critically examine claims about learning to recall and leverage as you interact with new ideas moving forward.

Step 1: Simply State the Claim (S)

You will find that most of the time when you hear about something that someone is selling an idea. That is not a bad thing (I'm proud to support capitalism but buyer beware!). But it is important when it comes to interacting with research because *how* something is presented has a significant effect on how we receive it. As such, your first step in interacting with any research is to get it down to the very basic, dry, assertion being made. At the most basic level in this first step is doing away with *framing effects*. We want to carefully consider what is stated and consider alternatives that say the same thing but frame it differently. For instance, consider statements A, B, C, and D for a school of 600 students as selling points for implementation of a new program:

 A. This program will ensure that 200 students will experience X
 B. There is a one-third probability that students will experience X
 C. Even after implementation of the program, 400 students will not experience X
 D. There is a two-thirds probability that students will not experience X

Every single one of these statements say the same thing. However, it is likely that you find Option A more appealing and that is because of framing effects. People who are advocating for something have often taken specific time and careful consideration to choose how it is framed. It is important to consider alternative framings because there is a well-established effect in which the way things are framed can skew how people respond to it. So, consider both and try to eliminate the influence of framing effects by stating it simply – or considering the alternatives. Everyone presents information that is framed in certain ways unconsciously – or intentionally. When you read a newspaper headline, very often it will skew your reading towards a particular interpretation. This is not all that different when reading and interacting with science. How a topic is framed can make it more or less likely that you will support its claims, independent of the evidence that exists for it. Here is a worked example and then we'll give you some basic guidelines for completing this first step.

Suppose I attend a conference and someone is presenting on learning styles and says that using her program of "Learning Styles to Improve Learning" will help your child thrive. Suppose she says the following in her persuasive presentation:

> All children have learning styles. There are some kids who learn kinesthetically, some who learn auditory, some who learn visually, some who learn logically – through math and numbers, and some who learn verbally. Using multiple learning styles and multiple intelligences for learning is a new and progressive approach. This approach is one that educators have only recently started to recognize. Traditional schooling uses linguistic and logical teaching methods. It also uses a limited range of learning and teaching techniques, which is really immoral when you think of schools' responsibility to teach all children! Many schools still rely on classroom and book-based teaching, much repetition, and pressured exams for reinforcement and review. A result is that we often label those who use these learning styles and techniques as bright. Those who use less favored learning styles often find themselves in lower classes, with various not-so-complimentary labels and sometimes lower quality teaching. This creates positive and negative spirals that reinforce the belief that one is "smart" or "dumb". By recognizing and understanding your own learning styles, you can use techniques better suited to you. This improves the speed and quality of your learning. If you find out what your child's learning style is and you teach them to it, you can unlock their true potential and will ensure that they get the most out of their learning[6]!

Before I dive into the worked example, I want to be clear that there are a lot of people peddling this idea of teaching to a students' preferred learning style to improve learning, but the overwhelming body of evidence does not support this claim. Pashler et al. (2009), in a wonderful synthesis of the research on learning styles used in an attempt to improve learning sum it up this way: "There is no adequate evidence base to justify incorporating learning-styles assessment into general educational practice" (p. 105). A nice analogy to contextualize this is that learning could be thought of as akin to "food" for your mind. As such, we might expect that there are things that are more and less healthy for us, just as is the case with food. And as we know, kids sometimes prefer things that are not as healthy for them. The same is true for learning – sometimes your preferred mode of learning is not the appropriate one to get the most out of it. The most nutritious learning style would be the one that is most likely to lead to greater learning based on the content and not personal preference.

Now, having ensured this inclusion would not confuse anyone into wasting their time with learning-styles assessments and tailoring lessons for a child's preference let's return to the task at hand. Let's cut the claim down to its bare bones to state it simply. The first action is that we want to *eliminate all the emotional aspects* embedded within. These emotional pieces are not, in and of themselves, evidence. Furthermore, they are powerful cues that can hinder our ability to focus on the facts at hand. So, looking back, we would cut out the phrases that focus on emotion including her claim about "using only a few of these as being immoral".

The next action in this first step is to identify *peripheral cues* in the message that tend to make us believe something, whether or not the evidence is there. This includes ideas that are familiar to us. We are much more likely to accept something if it is familiar. So be on the lookout for things that are familiar not to discount them but to put up a reminder to yourself that its familiarity is not sufficient for evidence! Another factor is ideas that are popular. If most of the people we surround ourselves with seem to believe something it is, again, more likely that we will accept it. But this is a form of social proof and is aptly labeled the "bandwagon" fallacy in logic. Again, this does not negate the idea at all, however, it is important to acknowledge that just because those who you are surrounded with tend to believe something is not scientific evidence at all. One more peripheral cue that can skew us from weighing the actual evidence is that we tend to believe things when they come from (a) people who we like or (b) people who see as "like us". In either case, we need to take note of that perception about someone because it typically means we also put our guard down for any skepticism about their claims. The goal in this first step is really about removing the idea from the perceptual factors that can skew our ability to interact with the idea itself.

These actions help to place ourselves in an objective stance towards the idea. Having done so, we next want to strip the overall claim to its basic central idea. In the example, the presenter includes a rant about problems in traditional schooling along with claims about her idea and a lot of inferences. So, how do we cut this down to size? Basically, the goal here is to say what is the basic claim that she offers and how is it presented? Is there another way it could be presented? A good strategy to attempt to reframe the presentation down to a simple and unloaded statement that takes the form of: "If I do X, Y will happen". So, looking back at her presentation, we could present her basic claim as: "If you teach your child in their preferred learning style, they will learn more". Great, now we've got it nailed down to a simple claim that we can consider without all the baggage.

To wrap up step one: Simply state the claim, here are the basic guidelines to employ at this step:

- Beware of the influence of *framing effects* – by considering it, as is, and through alternatives
- Eliminate ALL *emotion* from the claim
- Look out for *peripheral cues* that will distract us, and look like evidence but are not
  - Familiar Ideas
  - Popular Ideas
  - People we like
  - People who we think are like us

When all is said and done, this first step is an intentional effort to cut to the chase. In order to help us deal with new ideas, we need to eliminate the factors that can skew us from making an unbalanced decision. This is because the bottom line is that facts don't care about your feelings, but your feelings can impact how you interact with facts. Isaac Asimov is credited with having said: "Your assumptions are your windows on the world. Scrub them off every once in a while, to let the light in". I think that those two closing ideas recap this first step nicely. Gut the claim being considered down to exclude all emotional, peripheral, and framing effects to get as basic of an assertion about it as you can. From there, the subsequent steps will help you in coming to an objective decision about whether or not you should allow this new idea to inform your future practice.

Step 2: Examine the Authority (E)

Because someone is promoting an idea or program does not make them actually an expert in that area. There are many instances in which someone jumps into application (putting an idea into practice) without taking appropriate time to fully understand it or contemplate on its possible ramifications.

Ian Malcolm, in *Jurassic Park*, illustrated this beautifully when he criticizes Dr. Wu about his team's use of genetics to reconstruct dinosaurs in the fictitious and wonderful movie: "Yeah, but you were in such a hurry to see if you *could*, you didn't stop to think if you *should*!"

So, what are some factors you should look for about the person promoting an idea or program and the work that he bases his claims off of? I'll provide a checklist of factors to look at. The more you can check off, the better.

- Is the authority a person or just a word (e.g. science or research)?
  - If no, and the person promoting this says "science says" or "research says", ask for specific science or research and the authorities who produced it - this is critically important because science doesn't say anything; scientists do
  - If yes, consider the specific questions below to evaluate the relevance of his/her authority
- Does the authority share empirical evidence to support his or her claims?
  - If no, ask them for it (if they cannot provide any, it would be a red flag!)
  - If yes, take that evidence into consideration in step 3
- Does the authority have a terminal degree in the area that he or she is speaking about?
  - N.B. – A Ph.D. in Theoretical Physics is reasonably qualified to speak on theoretical physics, generally, however, in other areas he/she speculates (such as metaphysics) this status of expertise does not apply
- Does the authority have peer-reviewed publications on the topic at hand?
  - More is generally better in that it speaks to the author's competence and ability to convince other experts in the field of his arguments
- Is the authority recognized by others as an expert in the topic at hand?
  - This is the least helpful of these because it faces a kind of social proof challenge (that is, once interviewed as an expert, you are more likely to be interviewed as an expert)
- Is the person promoting this idea the original creator of it or is he building off of others?
  - If not, the initial authority it is extremely important to ensure they are not misrepresenting the original research (deeper emphasis in step 3 if he/she is not the original creator)

Step 3: Assess the Quality of Evidence (A)

The third step is the one that should take the most time because sometimes all we will have to work off of is the basic claims that a person is making. Many times, people are advocates for something but they do not have any evidence for it; it's just a hunch or a gut feeling. That does not make them wrong, but it makes them important to critically question. Furthermore, in the world of learning, there are many competing values and because it is a somewhat less mature science than other fields (such as cosmology, e.g.) there are also often competing views, even among experts. As such, this is the hinge point on which your critical examination of new findings must be scrutinized sincerely.

Scientific quality can break down at each of the three stages at which "good science" (observation, theorizing, and testing) can go bad. Observation is the first step in the scientific process and begins by picking a problem that can be observed and measured. Both of these can be critically examined. There are many things that we are interested in with regards to learning and student success that cannot be directly be observed. Consequently, most of the time we are using some "proxy" to measure what we are interested in. Take learning and creativity, for instance. Neither of these is something you *see*. Both require researchers (and teachers) to prod learners to gauge their "learning" or "creativity". As such, they have to develop instruments that they can use to measure these (called constructs). For instance, learning is typically measured by having students, without using notes/Internet, and so forth, respond to a series of questions that helps us to measure their learning in a subject. Creativity is also something that people have examined and have measured in varied forms. Some of the measures are better than others. To illustrate a poor proxy for creativity, I will introduce you to so-called divergent thinking tests. A common divergent thinking test is called the paperclip test. In this test, participants are asked to come up with as many uses of a paperclip as they can. Kids under the age of five have typically been able to come up with hundreds of uses, which according to their score is "genius" level. As people grow older, they are able to come up with less uses. A lot of advocates in the so-called 21st century learning groups point to divergent thinking tests to support their claim that schools kill creativity. This may be true but the evidence they point to in support of their claims is highly dubious. The fact that older persons identify less uses for a paperclip is primarily not because of a loss in creativity but the fact that they have more knowledge allowing them to filter out absurd ideas as being just that – absurd. When a child says a paperclip could be a space shuttle, it is cute and imaginative, but it is also ridiculous and thus, not a quality metric for productive creative thought. So, this is important. When we think about what research says, we need to know what is it that they are attempting to measure and how was it measured?

The second step in the scientific process is theorizing. The first thing to look for here is when a theory covers *everything*. If a theory accounts for all data, it is not a good thing; rather it is a fatal flaw to its viability for being a good theory in scientific research. For science, the focus is primarily on what is called "falsification". This makes reading research awkward at times, but it is built around a solid principle. Generally, it is pretty easy to find some corroborating evidence for an idea. So, if we are simply always looking for affirmative evidence for something, we can generally find something. But we are finite and will *never* be able to account for all instances, in all times, in all places, and in all contexts, et cetera. As science has accepted the idea that we cannot prove beyond the shadow of a doubt, it has adopted an approach that recognizes how we can use contradictory evidence to falsify claims and in doing so, consistently point us closer towards what is true. As such, you should be wary of anyone who points to evidence of all sorts and says: All of it is evidence for my theory. Chances are, that theory is nonsense. Now, when it comes to learning, I have provided for you a synthesis of the best evidence currently available and what it points to in Chapters One and Two in this book. As new theories are presented to you, reflect on the extent to which they make sense in light of the principles of learning outlined. If they do not fit with those, they will need to account for why those principles no longer hold[7] using evidence and not just theory because currently the best evidence available (and the preponderance of evidence) supports each of them overwhelmingly.

The final step in the simplified outline of the scientific process is testing. This is the point at which most criticism is likely to take place because the quality of a test determines whether or not there is any validity to inferences drawn from its data. In a nutshell, what we are talking about here is how the test was conducted (in research we call this methods or methodology). As noted earlier, it is forbidden for a scientist to keep his methods secret – he must reveal his playbook! Good science is public in that the researcher presents exactly what was done clearly such that it could be replicated in another setting and has his findings evaluated by peers (peer review process). Here is a short list of things to look for that could lead you to question the quality of a research study:

- **Quality of sample** (is the sample used in the study representative – that is, does it reflect closely the characteristics of the larger group it is trying to make claims about?)
- **Quality of participation** ([1] what proportion participated? If a significant percentage refused to participate, it suggests that we may

be missing something important and [2] if groups are compared and one group has a noticeably higher dropout rate than the other, it poses problems for legitimate comparison)
- **Quality of comparison**
  - If groups are not used, the study cannot make any claims of "x" is better than "y" – the only thing it can do is describe the results and connect it to others (like qualitative research)
  - If groups are used, each group should receive identical treatment aside from whatever is being tested (referred to as the intervention or independent variable) – the ideal case would include three groups – 1 receiving "x" treatment, 1 receiving "y" treatment, 1 receiving no treatment – in this way, meaningful comparisons can be made
  - If groups are used, each group should have its "scores" presented and the "variability of scores" (typically you'll see mean and standard deviation) – if the variability is very different between groups it suggests that comparison of means may be unjustified
- **Quality of objectivity** (as you read – or listen – do you detect obvious bias?)
  - Example 1: A researcher talks about lecture as "talking at", "sit and get", or "passive" – each of these demonstrates an overt bias against a lecture, if they were examining lecture, we have reason to wonder to what extent they presented it fairly
  - Example 2: A researcher explains that his goal is to challenge power structures – this is an obvious bias towards a preconceived truth that may or may not be true, it should be considered carefully because the researcher's mind is already made up, not because of the research but before the research because of his or her presuppositions
- **Quality of instruments** (how do they measure or collect data related to the variable(s) of interest? Are those good measures?)
  - Example 1: A researcher uses a personally created instrument (if he does not provide data on its reliability/validity it is worthy of questioning as meritorious)
  - Example 2: A researcher uses an existing instrument that has previously been checked for reliability and validity but in a different context (inappropriate unless rechecked for reliability and validity in this new context)
  - Example 3: Instruments that prioritize measures of objective data (actual performance, behavioral data, e.g.) is generally better than subjective data (self-report information, etc.)

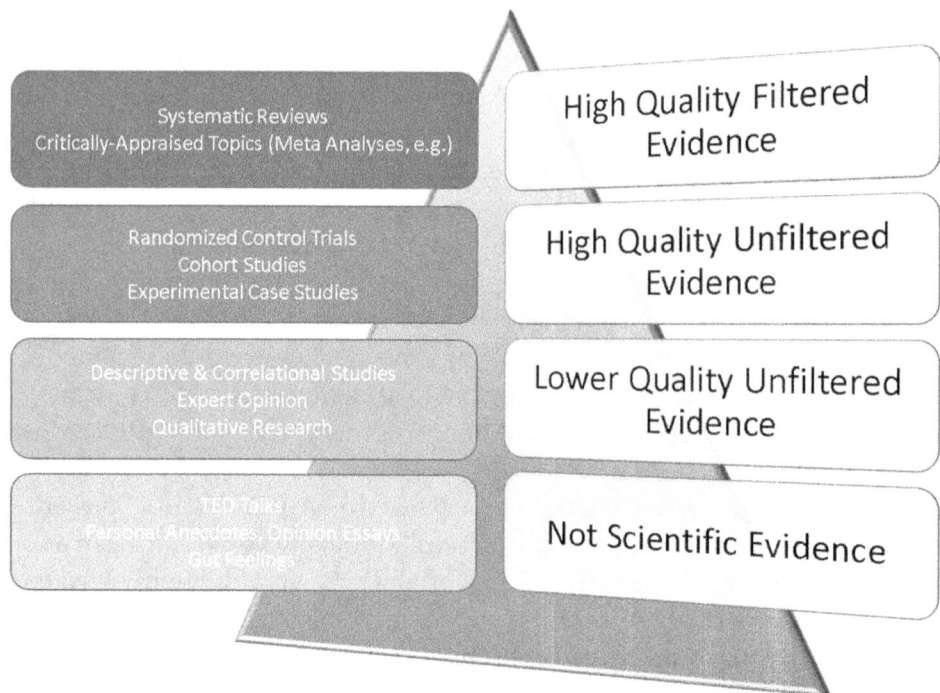

Figure 5.2 Hierarchy of evidence quality.

- **Quality of evidence** (weighted in line with Figure 5.2 with those at the top being stronger forms of evidence than those at the bottom[8] and please note that the top three layers are all evidence that we ought to draw upon, however, we ought to weight they accordingly)

Beyond those, there are other factors to consider. And again, here I'll provide a short list of bullet points to look out for so as to help you critically examine any such research/claims:

- **Absorb every fact; doubt every interpretation** (it is often difficult to differentiate between fact and inference, especially in a day when even major media organizations do not report facts but mostly present framed – and thereby inference-laden – coverage of facts. Distill through the flotsam of information and zero in on facts giving them priority while being skeptical of interpretations initially
- **Correlation does not imply causation** (if someone finds that two variables are related, he has no basis for claiming that he is aware of any causal relationship – doing so should discount his credibility)
- **Qualitative research is, by its nature, descriptive and should not be taken to imply causes** (anyone deriving causes from qualitative

inquiry should be questioned and we should look for the nuances the author themselves ought to clarify with regards to in what contexts these findings may have impact elsewhere)

- **Are there any omissions in the presentation of results** (how are charts organized – do they show appropriate ranges or is the way they are designed deceptive? Are you ever told the total sample size or do they only focus on percentages? This may mask a small sample size – Is there something interesting in the results that is not discussed in light of the major assertion? For instance, two tests may have been run with one being focused on because it had positive results – negative results are just as relevant but sometimes get pushed under the rug)
- **All research is based on assumptions, try to identify the researcher's assumptions** (we need to know what the researchers assume because if they assume something that is dubious, doubtful, or if something they assume alters how they report their findings, we have significant questions we must deal with regards to the study's quality and any inferences derived from it)

The last point on assumptions is particularly important in research because human beings are prone to confirming what they already believed. That is, as we interact with new information, it is constantly and uncontrollably done through a lens that basically wants to make new information fit with how we already view things. This is not necessarily a bad thing as it facilitates construction of schema, but we must be wary anytime we consistently find that we are proving what we already believed.

The ever-quotable Richard Feynman pointed out this problem for researchers by saying: "The first principle is you must not fool yourself, and you are the easiest person to fool"[9]. This is good advice for us to take, too, in that we need to proactively reflect on our own biases and assumptions or they will undoubtedly influence how we interpret things without our being aware of it. And that can be problematic for critical examination of just about anything! Finally, keep in mind that these steps – while they do follow a sequence – are part of a larger cycle and thus looking for other work on related topics is particularly crucial.

Step 4: Reflect on Conflicting Data Through Comparison (R)

Very often those who are peddling new ideas will focus only on evidence that supports their claim. You should request or actively seek out any conflicting evidence. Finding none makes it more important to focus back deeper in step 3, finding some mixed results you should simply put together a comparison table such as the example listed below in Table 5.2.

Table 5.2 Comparison of Research on 'X' Program

Study	Type of Study	Main Finding	Personal Rating
Title of Study 1 Here	Experimental, Correlational, Qualitative, Etc.	Look to the abstract, the primary assertion should be found there	Make up a rating scale (perhaps 0–5 with 5 being the highest quality, 0 being lowest quality)
Title of Study 2 Here	Continued	Continued	Continued
Title of Study 3 Here	Continued	Continued	Continued
Summary Results			

Your goal here is to reflect on steps 1–3 and give an overall rating to each study that looked at the same topic. A simple scale might be a rating of 0 for studies that do not meet many of the criteria herein up to 5 for those that seem to fit well with the quality factors I noted throughout steps 1–3. Finally, you would divide the total score (add up personal ratings of all studies and divide by the number of studies) to get an average. In doing so, you will get an aggregate score for all studies that have looked at the particular topic. If the average is near 4 or 5, you have pretty good reason to believe it, if the average is near 3, there is reason to remain somewhat skeptical, and anything below 3 would be something I would encourage avoiding currently because if the findings are based on shoddy work, we should probably be skeptical of their claims.

Step 5: Choose Whether It Is Worth Investing Resource in (CH)

The final step in this process is to weigh all that has been looked at and make a decision. Where does the bulk of the evidence lie? Does it fit with established evidence (again, consider Chapter One)? And don't forget the all-important question of does it matter? When all is said and done, if some new assertion is made but it does not have any immediate translation to improving the student and/or teacher's ability to make learning more efficient, it probably won't matter much. So, with some of those guiding questions in mind, reflect on the big picture and this overview of science. For when it comes to science and explanation, Richard Feynman perhaps summed it up best:

> "If it disagrees with experiment, it's wrong. In that simple statement is the key to science. It doesn't make a difference how beautiful your

guess is, it doesn't make a difference how smart you are, who made the guess, or what his name is. If it disagrees with experiment, it's wrong"[10].

Summary

We must avoid the all too common practice in educational circles of glorifying all that is new simply because it is new. If we ceaselessly celebrate and pursue all that is new and different simply because they appear "innovative", we dislocate ourselves from our conversation with the great ideas of the past and the distilled wisdom of the ages. We must engage with all that is new and innovative in education; but engagement cannot be done effectively without considering where we are, what we know (and have known), where we *could* go, and why we should do it? Those considerations require reflective consideration on past, present, and future – and in doing so, it provides a prudent approach to mapping the future for learning.

Equally, there are those on the other end who despise all that is new simply because it is new. This is an equally fallacious form of reasoning. Similarly, the failure to consider new ideas because they are new or based off ideas that one finds objectionable is akin to sticking your head in the sand and pretending the world is not all around you. A wise person will be judicious in consideration of old and new to critically examine what the best current evidence available might point us to in making the best decisions moving forward.

I am a firm advocate for taking advantage of all the benefits we are able to from the worlds of research and from technology. However, wading through the research and advocacy groups is easier said than done. So, I proposed a simple system through which you can stay engaged with current trends without (a) ignoring new ideas outright because they don't seem to fit and also without (b) getting caught up in the latest trend without scrutinizing it adequately.

So, in summary, there are five basic steps that we must do as we continue to interact with new ideas and claims related to the science of learning, which are outlined in Table 5.3 and organized around the mnemonic of S.E.A.R.CH. First, cut the claim down do its bare bones. Eliminate the emotion, consider how it is framed and alternatives, and identify peripheral cues such as familiarity that may skew my ability to critically examine the claim. Second, carefully examine the expert(s) making the claim. Are they an established and recognized authority in the field? Do they share evidence in direct support of their claims? Third, critique the scientific quality of studies that have looked at the idea and/or its claim. What assumptions are held by

Table 5.3 S.E.A.R.CH: 5 Steps to Interact with What Research Says

Step	Simple Description	Notes
1	Simply state the claim	Remove emotion, any framing language, and peripheral distractions so it is just a plain statement
2	Examine the authority	Determine their area of specialization, are they recognized by peers, do they present both sides fairly
3	Assess the quality of evidence	Look at the sample, the context, the measures used; consider the assumptions and rate overall quality
4	Reflect on conflicting data	Seek out evidence that may challenge the claim – compare them, considering quality of evidence
5	Choose if it should influence you	Weighing everything from above, make a decision as to if this is something worth investing in

the researchers? Are there groups being compared or is this merely descriptive? Are the measures used reasonable, accurate, and reliable? Does the evidence found allow for the inferences to made to be warranted? Fourth, compare conflicting evidence. Deliberately seek out possible alternative or contrary evidence and compare them to the evidence shared in support? Finally, based on your assessment of these four steps, wrap up with a fifth step of deciding whether or not it is worth modifying your approach to learning? Be sure to clarify what impacts you expect to find, pick a time and means to assess whether it is meeting your aims, and reassess the idea and its implementation at that time. I have provided a walkthrough checklist of key ideas derived from this section for engaging with new ideas/assertions in Appendix B.

This chapter presented a walkthrough for the alignment of best ideas of the past and best currently available evidence and a method for staying engaged as research progresses. Before moving into application, I want to extend upon some ideas that are commonly held in education that we should recognize as myths or outright nonsense. Because if we are drawn to their empty appeals, we will be hard-pressed to engage in serious thinking as we will allow erroneous ideas to become entrenched in our webs of understanding and they will damage our ability to critically examine new research. So, as you encounter all the persons who make the bold claim, "the research says!" remember to ask them, "what research" and then S.E.A.R.CH!

For Reflection and Application

Thinking back on this chapter, consider the following reflective tasks and ideas for application in your classroom:

1. List some peripheral cues that distract us from the actual quality of evidence. Have you seen any of these influence you, or others?
2. List some of the logical fallacies presented in the chapter. Find specific examples of these in popular media and consider sharing them with your students so that they start seeing "fallacious reasoning" and are less influenced by it.
3. What do each of the letters of the acrostic, *S.E.A.R.CH* stand for?
4. Look at a popular educational news outlet and some of its headline stories. Try applying this S.E.A.R.CH heuristic to interact with their claims.

Notes

1. From Eliot's essay, "Religion and Literature" placing emphasis on reading priorities.
2. That is, science as conducted in our contemporary world is unable to describe non-natural entities (such as God); the evidence collected from the natural world may guide our interpretation of what that means but it does not describe such entities in any way.
3. From Sir Arthur Conan Doyle's classic work, *Sherlock Holmes*.
4. Kendi, I. (2019). *How to be an anti-racist.* New York, NY: One World.
5. A great resource I have printed in my office comes from https://yourlogicalfallacyis.com/ - you might get one for yourself (they're free in PDF form)
6. This is made up by me, derived from a variety of online blog posts, articles, and so forth all advocating for teaching to a child's *preferred learning style*. I have adapted it slightly for the purposes of this step, too, of course, to ensure it serves as a good example!
7. As I noted in Chapter One, the principles I summarized are supported overwhelmingly by the best evidence we currently have in cognition. A change in those principles would be very unlikely and my suspicion is that anyone arguing against those would be doing so on the fact that they hold differing assumptions. You would have to get to what these are and weigh whether or not you found them more convincing to decide what to do with such a claim.

8. It is important to note that completing a quality meta-analysis in education is undoubtedly very difficult given the varied contextual factors involved in each unique study. Nonetheless, such large-scale analysis of high quality unfiltered evidence must certainly be taken seriously.
9. Feynman, Richard. (1985). *Surely, you're joking Mr. Feynman!* New York, NY: W.W. Norton & Company. Pg. 343.
10. Video clip from a lecture by Richard Feynman available on YouTube at: https://www.youtube.com/watch?v=b240PGCMwV0 – accessed 7/28/2018.

6

The 21st Century Trivium Framework

Thus far, we have surveyed essential principles to know about how learning occurs so that we make the many decisions we must make each day with them guiding as filters to the possible choices. Then, we looked at the trivium as a classical idea that offers a helpful look at how we might leverage those principles to promote learning that lasts. Finally, we took an excursus to carefully consider some common myths and nonsense we hear in education and how to engage with new ideas moving forward. Now, we are going to put the pieces all together into a systematic framework for learning. But before we present that framework, there is one last – and crucial element – we have to consider. We need to keep the ends in mind. Where is it that we are going? We need to clarify that so that our decisions coherently point us towards learning that is intentional.

Truth, Goodness, and Beauty

Schools are often pulled in many different directions – many of which demand using limited resources in contradictory ways. To help deal with this, the single best thing that we ought to do is to clarify exactly what our ends – or goals – are. Insofar as this book is interested, I've defined this for us – it is about student learning. There are many other popular goals, such as getting a job, providing food for students, developing self-esteem, promoting social justice, and so forth. These goals may or may not be laudable, but for the purposes of this book, each

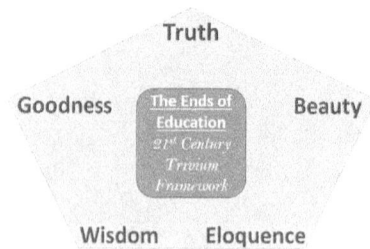

Figure 6.1 21st century trivium framework's ends of education.

of them distracts us from the primary purpose: Learning. So, if learning is our goal, is that it? No, I think we need to take a further step to clarify where that learning is directed towards. The 21st Century Framework will take on five points towards which our learning ought to be aimed. These include three enduring ideas of truth, goodness, and beauty and two ultimate traits we want to cultivate in our students: Wisdom and eloquence.

Figure 6.1 is a visual representation I have created to capture these essential ends of education that ought to serve as our guide in what we want for our education to lead towards (its ends). In terms of topics, our learners pursue truth, goodness, and beauty and in terms of traits we want to cultivate wisdom and eloquence.

So, following the 21st century Trivium framework, our purposes are the pursuit of truth, the cultivation of the good, and the admiration and evaluation of the beautiful culminating in the development of wisdom and eloquence. In the contentious world in which we live, simply framing these as our ends allow for people who disagree on virtually everything to engage in meaningful and respectful discussion and pave the pathway to a future in which civil disagreement can move in a positive direction.

Truth

When all is said and done, our view of truth may very well be the single most important view we have for how we interact with the rest of the world. Generally speaking, there are four primary views of truth, which I have displayed in Figure 6.2 below, adapted from another of my books: *The Decay of Truth in Education*[1].

A quick summary of the various perspectives we can have with regards to truth follow:

- **Correspondence View** – truth is that which corresponds to reality; facts and evidence are necessary to support what is true; something cannot be both true and false in the same context
- **Critical View** – truth is socially negotiated/constructed and is also used by the powerful to maintain their positions of power
- **Pragmatic View** – truth is what works; it doesn't really matter if something is objectively true, what is of interest is what helps us in the moment
- **Relativistic View** – truth is subjective; there is no truth, only perspective; something can be true for one person but not for another

The 21st Century Trivium Framework ◆ 87

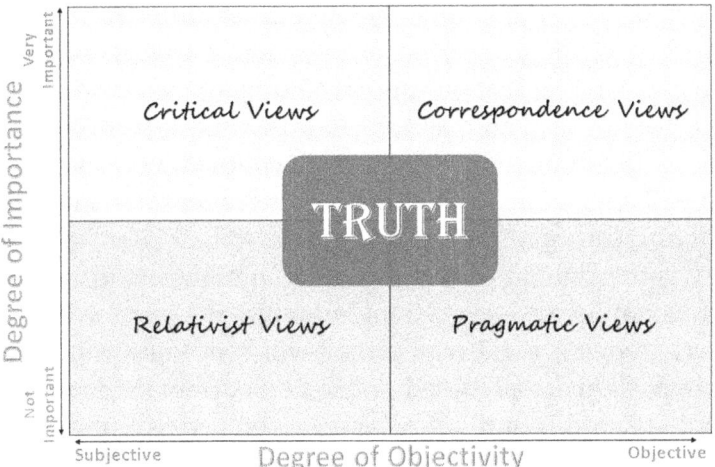

Figure 6.2 Competing views of truth.

Just a short read of those bulleted summaries and you no doubt saw elements of each of those in things you believe, have heard, and see on a daily basis. Our society is one that both largely holds to and, paradoxically, has largely abandoned the correspondence view. This poses significant problems for learning as I argue in *The Decay of Truth in Education*. To sum up some of the important points for our purposes here, in its wake, these other views of truth have filled the gaps leading to a wide variety of completely contradictory views being held by individuals. Furthermore, depending on the perspective and political activism of the individual, some (critical views) tend towards extremism and totalitarianism making us ripe for deception, while others (pragmatic and relativistic views) tend toward disengagement, and makes us ripe for distraction and delusion (relativistic views). Only the correspondence view with its commitment to the laws of identity (A=A) and law of non-contradiction (A cannot be both A and non-A in the same sense and in the same context) do we have a view of truth that is worthy for an education. Insofar as you operate in your classroom, you likely adhere to classic elements of this correspondence view:

- Your assessments try to measure, accurately, what you attempt to evaluate
- Your grades try to measure, accurately, student learning
- Your lessons try to help students engage with specific learning outcomes you hope they learn

Since these are true for each of us, we should advocate specifically for the pursuit of truth bound to the correspondence understanding. That means we should be explicit to our students that, in our learning, our aim is always to get as close as possible to understanding what is true. This means that we should also make it clear that our understanding of the world is always based on the evidence we have and, as such, our pursuit of truth is never ceasing. This sense of a commitment to pursue truth coupled with an affirmation that the pursuit will not end in our lifetime here is the foundation for the singular best aim for our learning.

So, why is the pursuit of truth such an important and primary aim for learning? It is not because everything our students learn in our classes will be absolutely true, nor is it because they will ever know all truth. Rather, it is because to recognize that, based on the best current evidence, their understanding of the world is built off what is recognized as true. This is critically important because it both humbles and expands the mind. When we recognize that we are finite and that our learning can never be exhaustive, we are ready to acknowledge our limits and yet we are also motivated to get as close to right as possible. If we are drawn away from a correspondence view of truth towards any of these other perspectives, we will also lose these virtues and increase the potential influence of distraction, deception, and delusion on our learners.

Goodness

On one hand, there are those who will see the inclusion of goodness and think – hold on, we can't teach morality in school! To that, I would reply: Nonsense. Every educational experience teaches – implicitly or explicitly – morals. When a school puts a policy in place mandating that people use particular language, they are putting a moral policy in place. When a teacher establishes a rule that must be followed, he or she is regulating behavior. Guess what? Every single policy, procedure, and routine we put into place – or fail to put into place – has one of three effects on behavior. It is either passive on a behavior, thereby permitting it; it is restrictive on a behavior, thereby prohibiting it; or it is encouraging towards a behavior, thereby promoting it. So, if you have any single policy or procedure in your school or classroom, guess what? You're already teaching a particular sense of morality. So, with that put aside, let's look at what this means in the context of the classroom and learning in any domain.

What I mean when I discuss goodness is that we cannot passively engage with our domains, we need to think about the big questions. We must have discussions of what is right and wrong or what is good and evil. In some instances, it is reasonable that all students will come to a similar consensus: Such as that National Socialism and Communism are reprehensible ideologies that have wrought horrendous consequences on humanity. In other instances, however, students will engage with ideas that are not so crystal clear and we want to cultivate the capacity in our students to interact with persons whom they disagree, respectfully. If students are not reasonably trained to discuss and engage with ideas of goodness, they may not ever have the opportunity to recognize nuance and respect persons as being able to reasonably come to different views on controversial topics. When we engage as humans in learning, we are engaging in the millennia-long conversation around great ideas and considering what is good is a central piece for decisions that govern our daily lives. As such, purposeful consideration of goodness within the educational project is a second aim for our learning. So, you ought to encourage your students to consider what is good and how we are best to be good in light of relevant topics in your domain. This is undoubtedly a critically important purpose of education. As G.K. Chesterton wrote over a century ago, "education is simply the soul of a society as it passes from one generation to another". Ultimately, a healthy engagement with consideration of what is good is an important part of what we want to pass on to the next generation – not necessarily exactly what is good but that we value goodness and its pursuit must be continued as part of the ends of becoming an educated person.

Beauty

Beauty is one of the factors that really makes humans stand apart. No other lifeform, that we are aware of, takes any notice of beauty or is struck asunder by looking upon something, mesmerized by its "beauty". As such, it is an important aim to cultivate as we learn. However, people often tend to confuse beauty as solely being based on a person's opinion. In fact, we often hear this when people say, "beauty is in the eye of the beholder". This, however, is something the 21st century trivium approach to education will intentionally take on. It is vital to distinguish between beauty and "I like" something. Our like or feeling towards something does not determine its beauty. It is simply a reflection of our preferences.

The ancient Roman architect Vitruvius provides a classical conception of beauty including emphasis on complexity with underlying unity:

> Architecture consists of Order … and arrangement … and of proportion and symmetry and décor and distribution … Order is the balanced adjustment of the details of the work separately, and as to the whole, the arrangement of the proportion with a view to a symmetrical result (Vitruvius, 1970, 26–27).

St. Thomas Aquinas in *Summa Theologica*, defines beauty as embodying three characteristics: (1) Wholeness, (2) proportion, and (3) radiance (I. 39.8). So, we might say that integrity, balance, and clarity form a classical understanding of beauty. There is also an idealistic sense of beauty that speaks to a connection between a product and observers that unites them in a way and links universality and particularity as articulated by Hegel (1835).

But beauty is deeper than simply a list of characteristics, too. There is something embedded that provides a sense of a more complex form of beauty. For instance, a person may be physically beautiful but they have some trait that detracts from, or enhances, their beauty. The inner traits of something – often related to truth or goodness – allow us to understand a deeper aspect of complex beauty. At its core, the aim of beauty as a target for education demands that we slow down and observe a product to examine it more holistically. Observation means to inspect and take note of; to look carefully with attention to detail. In Sir Arthur Conan Doyle's Sherlock Holmes series, Sherlock would often correct his friend by saying, "Watson, you see but you do not observe".

One of the great disservices we do to our youth is that we fail to acknowledge the beauty and wonder we experience in everyday life. C.S. Lewis once remarked that reason is the organ of truth and imagination is the organ of meaning, arguing that both must be cultivated. Knowledge of something that is true is important but "knowledge of" can exist without meaning and if Lewis is right, perhaps we ought to be more explicit in cultivating a sense of wonder and curiosity in our students as meaning-enhancing tool. In fact, this is one of the most important elements for aiming learners towards beauty – seeing the wonder in nature, in the constructions of mankind, and in our basic humanity is an essential element for fostering in learners a prudent judgment of the beautiful.

Our world is filled with natural beauty, human history is littered with beautiful creations, and the least we can do in a meaningful educational experience is to pursue it actively. This is especially the case in our present age that is so drawn to rushing through everything to simply get to the next box to check off our lists. Beauty calls us to pause, to linger, to immerse ourselves in, and to contemplate on things that matter. My wife often tells a story that is worth considering in this context. When she was younger, her family traveled from their home in Phoenix to the Grand Canyon. From the Phoenix area, this is quite a long drive (almost four hours). She recalls that upon arriving, her family took little more than a few minutes to look around and say: "Well there it is, the Grand Canyon!" After posing for a few pictures and taking a couple more of the view, her parents said, "Let's go! We've got to get on the road to be back in time for dinner". If we fail to inculcate a desire to pursue beauty in our children, this will likely be their fate. They will fail to recognize the beauty that is right in front of them while they rush to what's next on the agenda. For many who do not pause to reflect on and admire the beauty all around us, it is almost like they live in a drive-by existence. They say that they have "experienced" something because they have seen it, but in reality, all they have done is that they have been exposed to it, at most. True experience requires time to immerse, to ponder, to reflect, and to admire what is beautiful in each domain.

A famous account of Sir William Osler, who was a professor of medicine at Oxford University, underscores the distinction between observation and seeing and/or having experienced something. At one lesson, he wanted to emphasize the importance of attention to detail in observation so he announced to his class that he had a bottle of urine for analysis. He told them that it's often possible to determine the disease from which a patient suffers if we observe the details. He dipped a finger into the fluid and brought it out, then placing a finger into his mouth. He continued speaking and passed the bottle around instructing students to do exactly as he had done. The bottle made its way around, with each student cringing and sampling the contents with a frown. When the bottle had reached everyone, it came back to Dr. Osler who said, "Gentlemen, now you will understand what I mean when I speak about details. Had you been observant, you would have seen that I put my index finger in the bottle but my middle finger into my mouth!" This was likely a lesson his students never forgot!

Osler said that there is no more difficult art to acquire than the art of observation. A commitment to pursue and study beauty demands a slowing down, extended observation, a careful attention to detail, and an appreciation for precision, in addition to embracing a unique element of our humanity. Beauty is, thus, the third big aim for our learning as it demands that we be willing to slow down and embrace our human desire to see that which is beautiful and study things in depth. So, truth, goodness, and beauty offer us healthy, universal ends for our learning by focusing what we want to learn about within each domain. But that is not all.

Wisdom and Eloquence

When we think about ends, we need to consider the transcendent aims that shape our learning but we also need to think about the pragmatic aims. When students leave our tutelage, our stamp will be on them – for better or worse. So, what traits seem universally relevant that also can help us keep our decision-making, moving learners towards that end? My response to this question is that wisdom and eloquence, especially in our times, stand out as crucial.

The world in which we live is one that has been labeled a "post-truth" and "post-modern" society. In large part, I would argue that because of our shift in the past few decades towards a society of information overload, there is more risk now for distraction, for deception, and delusion than at any other point in human history. In combating these significant risks, we need to train our students to be eloquent speakers who are equipped with the knowledge, precision, and skill to persuade others amongst the cacophony of competing, and often contradictory, voices. Furthermore, our students must be equipped with a heavy dose of humility, of experience – drawn from personal application and from the rich store of historical experience of societies, such that they are wise about when and how to engage. As such, it is in our particular contextual circumstances that wisdom and eloquence are two aims that must be considered as primary among our educational purposes. And among these, wisdom is primary. Eloquence, without wisdom, can be leveraged by charlatans to persuade others. And in the world in which we live, with such widespread deception, delusion, and distraction, many are trained to be eloquent but use that prowess in persuasion for ill ends. Wisdom is the necessary precursor to an appropriate training in eloquence – we cannot equip frauds to take over from their smooth speech; rather we must equip our students with wisdom first and then eloquence that they might meet them in the marketplace of ideas and lead us in appropriate directions.

How then, might one go about developing wisdom? Perhaps the single best presentation of the steps to wisdom are articulated by Augustine in *On Christian Doctrine*. He outlines six steps to wisdom in a distinctly Christian sense and it is worth examining, after which I will synthesize these into a secular version of the steps to wisdom. For Augustine, the first step is *fear*. We begin through fear of the Lord and recognizing that we are finite and fallible and that we will stand before the judge of the universe. Said directly, the first step is to throw away our pride. The second step is *piety*. Putting your trust into Scripture and immersing yourself into it is the necessary aspect of piety. The third step is *knowledge*. Acquisition of knowledge requires an earnest study of the Word of God for He is to be loved for His own sake. Furthermore, the Christian is commissioned to love God with all their heart, all their soul, all their body, and all their mind. The fourth step on the path to wisdom is *strength and resolution*. This is not a quick process; there is not a shortcut. Augustine explains that we must steadfastly pursue righteousness and fix our thoughts on those things that are eternal, not transient. The fifth step, then is cultivating a *counsel of compassion*. He suggests this requires cleansing the soul. Adhere to the second greatest commandment: To love your neighbor as yourself and to see your enemy as God does – as a unique child of God.

Table 6.1 Krahenbuhl's Steps to Learn for Wisdom (Adapted from Augustine)

The Pathway on Learning for Wisdom	
1. Fear	<ul><li>Acknowledge your own ignorance and inability to know it all</li><li>Humble yourself; give up your pride</li><li>Desire to learn for learning's sake</li></ul>
2. Piety	<ul><li>Put your trust to grow in wisdom by diving into the field</li><li>Immerse yourself in the established body of research</li></ul>
3. Knowledge	<ul><li>Carefully examine the literature of the field</li><li>Examine developments in the field</li><li>Respect their giant shoulders on which we stand</li></ul>
4. Strength & Resolution	<ul><li>Hold the long view – short term/anecdotal is less significant than trends</li><li>Fix your mind on seeking a careful, nuanced, and *accurate* understanding</li></ul>
5. Counsel of Compassion	<ul><li>Do not permit yourself to caricature</li><li>Understand other views in their best light; as their advocates do</li></ul>
6. Purification	<ul><li>Understand the field as it truly is</li><li>Your understanding broadens and your path to wisdom is under way</li></ul>
Finally, we arrive at wisdom	

Finally, the sixth step to wisdom is *purification*. Through this process, the soul is purified and one can see God as He truly is. Now, the person is equipped for wisdom.

Augustine's brilliant articulation of this process that leads to wisdom is one that we can adopt in any field or domain, as well. Table 6.1 presents my own reconceptualization of this that can be leveraged into any discipline – be it religious or secular.

An ultimate end of education is that learners who leave our guidance are equipped and able to engage with the world around them. Of central importance then, is the ability to communicate effectively. Eloquence is, however, more than just quality communication. Eloquence conveys a rich sense of fluency and precision that encompasses understanding. That is, an eloquent communicator is one who effectively adheres to some classic advice from Aristotle: The wise man speaks when he has something to say; the fool speaks because he has to say something. Our eloquent communicators who have developed wisdom through a steadfast pursuit of truth, consideration of goodness and beauty, and cultivation of eloquence will be equipped to speak when he or she is able and to do so in nuanced and articulate manner. He or she will not fall into the trap that too many youths today are forced into as they are compelled to speak well before they understand and thus, before they ought to speak.

So, our idealistic ends are targeted towards truth, goodness, and beauty; and our pragmatic ends are to cultivate wisdom and eloquence. This framework is purposefully tipped towards the idealistic ends so that they are primary. What is expedient works for the moment; it is immediate, impulsive, and incredibly limited and so we need to have aims bigger than the moment itself. Keeping the five ends that we have laid out here will protect us from the constant flux of seeking expedient. Of course, our goals are to equip learners with knowledge and skill to engage in the real world which means they will necessarily engage in issues of the moment. But through this slightly tipped balance towards idealistic, with a healthy focus on the pragmatic, we equip our learners with the core of what it means to be wise. A wise person holds the long view but is able to apply that in making decisions about how to deal with reality.

Students must leave our school, our classroom, and/or our domain equipped with a rich body of knowledge, with a sense of curiosity to know more, with a humble awareness of their own strengths and weaknesses, a passion for truth and accuracy, a compassionate commitment towards doing good, and a desire to seek what is beautiful but also must be capable of engaging in meaningful conversation in a world that is increasingly giving itself up to distraction, deception, and delusion. So, at the school level, at the classroom level, and within your primary spheres of influence take on these aims for education: Truth, goodness, beauty, wisdom, and eloquence.

The 21st Century Trivium Framework for Learning

Now we have everything in place to unveil the 21st Century Trivium Framework. Figure 6.3 provides the visual illustration of this framework.

The foundations are the essential base on which the framework rests. And this foundation was laid through a systematic reflection on the best current evidence we have with regards to how people learn since learning is the fundamental purpose of education. As such, our foundation includes two essential bases: Principles for engaging learning and principles for enhancing learning. These foundations underlie everything we do. What this means for practice is that all our decisions ought to be filtered through them.

The pillars that we rest upon these foundations are derived from classical education and include the three stages of learning articulated in the

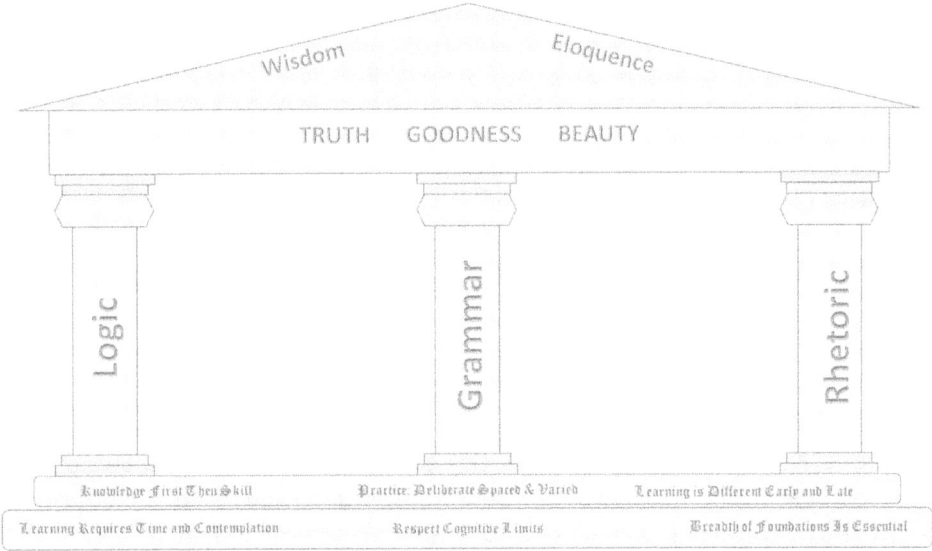

Figure 6.3 The 21st century trivium framework.

trivium: Grammar, logic, and rhetoric. These stages were presented as a helpful way to visualize the process of learning, which, while not linear, is enhanced by intentional design. Grammar is found as the central pillar in our framework because it is the vital starting point for learning in any area. First, we must understand the basic essential knowledge and the rules that govern that area. From there, we can move through logic and rhetoric stages to challenge learners to engage with competing understandings, examining rules and patterns, to tighten up more coherent understanding, and to, when equipped, express oneself elegantly in the domain.

Finally, we have in this chapter laid the peak of our framework in our educational ends. As our students move through their experience of learning, they are engaging with the great ideas that make humans unique. Their learning is constantly in the pursuit of truth, considers the implications of what they learn for what it means to be good and for what is beautiful, and it is our intention that they leave, as learners engaged through this framework, as wise and eloquent persons.

Four Strategies to Implement

Before we turn to specific instructional applications and content area applications, let me present four strategies to implement in your context that are derived from this framework. Each of these is designed to promote a truth-focused, goodness and beauty seeking, wise journeyer who is on a great quest for learning.

Cultivate Wonder and Creativity

Perhaps the most obvious method for fostering the imagination is through the power of stories. Through stories, we can help our learners recognize not only what is true, but we can facilitate meaningful discussion about what is good, what is beautiful, what is worthy of admiration, and so forth. As Kieran Egan (2005) describes:

> Stories are instruments for orienting human emotions to their contents. That is, stories do not just convey information about events and characters, nor do stories just convey information in a way that engages our emotions; stories *orient*, or shape, our emotions to the events and characters in a particular way – they tell us how to feel about their contents (p. 10).

The story facilitates a conversation that can contextualize these truths and enrich learning by developing meaning. This enhances both recall of information and also provides a way to help engage learners in important questions about truth, goodness, and beauty, orienting their feelings towards these ends rather than simply understanding material.

I was at a presentation in Cincinnati, Ohio where I was inspired to write this piece by a series of writers and speakers. One of them, N.D. Wilson, provided one of the most wonderful examples of the power of recasting what is true in beautiful story form to cultivate a sense of wonder. In his presentation, he gave a series of such illustrations, one of which is retold below as an example. Wilson explained that when learning science, we put it in such dry terms that miss the wonder of the world in which we live that it is no wonder that kids wished they lived in *Middle Earth* or *Tatooine* or *Hogwartz*[2] instead of here. But *here* is in many ways even more amazing – because the amazing happens every day and it is *real*! He illustrated our callousness to the wonder in our world by sharing that: "We live on a huge mass of rock, water, and lava that floats around a massive burning ball of fire moving at eighty-six times the speed of sound, all while acting like nothing special is going on![3] What a brilliant and honest reflection on our all-too-common apathy towards the natural world. We can learn from his beautiful illustration that as educators we ought to slow down, reflect, and admire the wonder that surrounds us.

Find meaningful opportunities to point out the beauty and wonder in our world and rip off our callousness towards them. From the micro level such as the incredible design and efficiency of DNA to the macro level of the earth and cosmos, present the facts, but take a moment to reflect on and wonder at the amazing things that surround us. We must hold truth in high esteem but ought to present it in beautiful story form to inspire others to not just be observers of the world but to recognize themselves as active characters in it. We live in a world of beauty, of wonder, and of truth – let us intentionally cultivate a sense of curiosity and reverence for this amazing gift of life that we are given. Try to think of topics in your area and tell the truths in engaging, story form.

Engage Controversial Topics in Your Domain
In virtually every domain, there are many different perspectives on what is best, on what is right, and on what is beautiful. These areas must be leveraged as the interaction with such divergence allows for a meaningful interaction between all three stages of the trivium that will fuel their creativity as they imagine the possibilities. To put it simply, find topics that include controversy in your domain – or that at a minimum contain compelling contrasting perspectives on something.

Begin by having the class be introduced to the controversial topic through a compelling question or perhaps a juxtaposition of seemingly contradictory claims. This ought to pique their interest and focus them into the area into which we will be exploring. Next, sufficient time must be put in place to ensure that students acquire sufficient background knowledge for the controversy *and* they must understand both perspectives accurately, albeit basically. At this point, the students must explore the controversial topic and the sides that are defended enough that they can *articulate each side accurately and persuasively*. As John Stuart Mill stated in *On Liberty*:

> He who knows only his own side of the case knows little of that. His reasons may be good, and no one may have been able to refute them. But if he is equally unable to refute the reasons on the opposite side, if he does not so much as know what they are, he has no ground for preferring either opinion … Nor is it enough that he should hear the opinions of adversaries from his own teachers, presented as they state them, and accompanied by what they offer as refutations. He must be able to hear them from persons who actually believe them … he must know them in their most plausible and persuasive form.

During this phase of articulation, the end goal is that the student actually understands both sides of the controversy as they would be presented in their most persuasive form – not as caricatured presentations. This is no easy task but is essential in cultivating curiosity because if either alternative is presented in a weak form, there really is no debate and it's simply an exercise in polemics. And as Aristotle suggested over two millennia ago, "the mark of an educated person is to entertain an idea without accepting it". Doing this with controversial issues brings the current world into learning and does so in a way that places primacy not on pontification but on humble understanding. That will no doubt improve civil society in the long-run as we will be fast to listen and slow to speak, which is about the exact opposite of much of what seems to be prioritized today which encourages spouting off uninformed views as often and as loudly as possible to "facilitate personal meaning-making", which only internalizes biases and enhances tribalism causing damage to civility.

Having reached this point in engaging with the controversial idea through this 21st Century Trivium-informed manner, you are ready to take the controversy to its culmination. Students ought to be required to pick a side and prepare a defense of it. Furthermore, they must be cross-examined by others who are committed critics – or at least play the role of them informed by sufficient preparation as would be in place if the second stage was completed correctly. A compelling and rigorous debate in the classroom on such controversial issues in the domain will ensure that students recognize their own humility, recognize the areas in the field where investigation is ongoing, and will promote their curiosity as to what is next and their creativity to imagine what is possible?

Promote a "What If" and "Maybe" Mindset
All too often, however, we in schools do not cultivate a mindset that favors asking "what if" and "maybe". There are many factors that tend us towards that unfortunate reality. Often, we feel pressured to teach to the test and do not want to offer the time to engage in such intellectual wandering. Sometimes we have good reasons for being cautious about this but let them stop us from pursuing it all together. For instance, in a classroom where students are not equipped with sufficient knowledge, they are likely to ask questions that are insignificant, off-topic, and distracting. In such an environment, it is probably wise to avoid cultivating this sort of mindset because you are letting the blind lead the blind. However, if you are adhering to principles embedded throughout this book, that is not something you will need to worry about. Rather, your students will be sufficiently equipped with the background knowledge to pose questions that you may not have thought of, to offer "what if" and "maybe" possibilities that will fuel their wonder and curiosity in the domain as well as encourage them to keep learning. My colleague and I have developed a framework to cultivate creativity called

Signature Thinking and this "what if and maybe mindset" is one of its essential components[4].

It should never be forgotten that learning does not stop when learners leave our classroom. Cultivating a mindset in your students that tends them to prioritize acquiring knowledge about the domain and then consistently asking "what if" and "maybe" will well prepare them for a few essential tools for lifelong learning. Once they leave your tutelage, will they still wonder about your subject matter? Through promoting these types of questions, you will make it so more often than not, they will.

Lectio Divina for Any Classroom

Lectio divina is a traditional monastic practice formalized by St. Benedict of Nursia to promote a sincere attempt to understand scripture as God intends it to be understood. *Lectio divina* consists of four steps: (1) Reading scripture, (2) meditating on scripture, (3) offering prayers to God for guidance to His intended meaning rather than our own, and (4) contemplation upon the scripture and its implications. Let me attempt to translate this to something you can do immediately in a public – or any classroom – while engaging with high quality, text-based material.

Begin with preparation. Start students and yourself off in silence and reflection on what is about to be examined. This helps us focus on our aim – not our personal opinion but on understanding what the text intends to say. Next, implement step one: Read the text. A collective read is worthwhile. Be interactive with reading, pay careful attention to the precise words of the text, and seek to understand the text – on *its terms*. Then, move to step two: Meditation on the text. Think on the actual words of the text itself, record questions you think of, things you noticed about the words and text, and start to ponder the question: What does the text mean? It is important at this point to note that the goal in this stage is not to assign meaning to the text. The emphasis of meditation is always the text itself and not ourselves. The third step is prayer in the *lectio divina* tradition with the aim of allowing God to guide your understanding. Clearly, in a secular classroom, we will not be asking students to let the Holy Spirit guide them! The point here is to lean on the authority – in our classroom, that is you, the teacher. Guide them through a reflective interaction with the text. In our classroom, then, a good model might be to provide everyone a short one-half page handout asking the questions outlined in Table 6.2 below.

Having spent a good bit of time meditating on the text, we move to step four: Contemplation. Finally, we contemplate on the text, reflect back on the dialogue we have had with the author, consider the questions we have posed and attempted to answer, and finally begin to think about what the text

Table 6.2 Questions to Meditate – Think Deeply About Text

Question	Purpose
What is the topic at hand?	Knowing the primary topic is a first, important step to accurate interpretation
Does the author use any specific words that I do not understand?	Identify words that we don't know to define them – Words that are not understood make interpretation much more difficult (more complicated if using historical texts where meanings can mean different things than they do today)
Do I notice any important, cueing words?	Look for words that cue us to where we need to look to try and understand the intended meaning (example: therefore/however each point us back to something)
What words seem particular important?	Focus on precision – people choose their words carefully when writing, each one matters and we should demand our students focus on this level of precision down the very words on the page
What do we know about the historical context in which this was written? (if applicable)	Focus on empathy – people have a tendency to engage in chronological snobbery (that is, we think we're so much better than those in the past) – stay humble and recall that all of us are largely influenced by the cultural milieu in which we live

means in the context of what you're seeking. Here are some contemplative things you might think about having reached this last step:

- If I had been sitting with the author face-to-face, what would I ask him or her?
- Is there some larger truth the author is trying to convey?
- Is the text teaching a moral?
- Is there something noticeable in the author's choice of words that points towards deeper meaning?
- Is there something structural that underscores an attempt to make a passage especially beautiful?
- Is there something in today's world that meaningfully connects to the topic the author is discussing?

Be at peace knowing you will not unravel everything. But confident that through this process you have committed yourself, purposefully, to taking the path towards wisdom that runs through the ends of truth, goodness, and beauty.

Summary

Neil Postman (2005), author of *Amusing Ourselves to Death*, offers up three commandments that all video producers adhere to (whether they know it or not), which underscore some of the problems of contemporary education. His three commandments these videographers discouragingly adhere to include: (1) *Thou shalt have no prerequisites*; (2) *thou shalt induce no perplexity*; and (3) *thou shalt avoid exposition like the ten plagues visited upon Egypt*. Through adhering to these three commitments, Postman argues that television (in large doses) dulls the mind and makes one less capable of engaging in contemplation and deep thought. You no doubt see parallels to much of our contemporary educational system through these three commandments. Everything in education seems to be so focused on the individual that the emphasis is for immediate application, always seeing everything in a personal context, and certainly not valuing the long hard-work that comes with the practice necessary to memorize information. In other words, our contemporary educational system adheres to these commandments in a great deal of what it does. Unfortunately, Postman explains: "The name we may properly give to an education without prerequisites, perplexity, and exposition is *entertainment*" (p. 148 – emphasis added).

In this chapter, we have introduced the 21st Century Trivium Framework. The foundation of our framework rests upon principles of learning. These broad axioms should guide all our decision-making in promoting learning. The pillars of our framework include the three stages of the trivium – grammar, logic, and rhetoric. The intentional movement through these in your learning environment systematically moves learners towards our ends. And the ends we provided in this chapter helped shape the peak to our framework. Our learning is directed towards the pursuit of truth, the consideration of goodness, the admiration of beauty, the cultivation of wisdom, and the culminating task of eloquence. Finally, I presented four specific strategies derived from this framework that are encouraged to implement into your context. Next, we will think about what adopting this framework means for application. What implications does this offer for instruction? What guidance and specific examples can be offered in primary content areas?

For Reflection and Application

Thinking back on this chapter, consider the following reflective tasks and ideas for application in your classroom:

1. Think of the essential components of the 21st Century Trivium Framework: A Foundation of Principles for Learning; pillars outlining a process for engaging learners; and a peak focused on the ultimate ends of learning. Sketch some notes about what this looks like in your content area(s).
2. Print off Krahenbuhl's 21st Century Trivium Framework and put it in your classroom somewhere to serve as a reminder of our foundation, our phases, and our ends.
3. Which of the four strategies do you see the best opportunity to put into practice in your classroom immediately? What resources should you assemble to integrate that into your instruction?

Notes

1. Here is a link to a freely available read of the Introduction and Chapter One of this book should you be interested to dive more deeply into an argument for restoring truth as paramount in education: https://www.cambridgescholars.com/download/sample/64328
2. References to Lord of the Rings, Star Wars, and Harry Potter, respectively.
3. For reference, the speed of sound (at 68 degrees F) is 768.2 mph; Earth spins (rotates) at 1,000 mph at the equator; Earth moves (orbits the sun) at around 67,000 mph. So, on earth – right now – you are spinning *faster than the speed of sound* and *are moving at approximately 87 times it* and yet we have no idea we are moving that fast!
4. Krahenbuhl, K.S. & Carter, J.L. (2018). *The signature thinking framework: Cultivating productive creativity in history*. Proceedings of the Midwestern Educational Research Association, Presented in Cincinnati, Ohio.

7

Instructional Principles

Instructional design and delivery are crucially important factors in shaping the environment for learning in ways that do not leave learning to chance but rather, are designed for learning. We ought to hold to a healthy humility against our tendency to overestimate how well we know something simply because we have learned about it. Flannery O'Connor eloquently made this point by noting: "I have what passes for an education in this day and time; but I am not deceived by it". Likewise, we have had an education and continue in our own education but we cannot let that delude us with thinking that we know everything that we need to know. We want to maintain a sense of humility in what we do for to draw upon the science of learning to impact the art of teaching takes a delicate balance of wisdom, prudence, patience, and humility.

In this chapter I will articulate specific elements we can draw upon from cognitive science and the classical model for learning so that we establish a clear 21st century trivium approach to building effective learning environments. Leveraging the empirical data and time-tested wisdom of this synthesized approach will equip you to maximize your effectiveness and the impact you have on your learners.

The Benefit of Grammar, Logic, and Rhetoric as Stages

It is important to note that the trivium (grammar, logic, and rhetoric) have not always been understood as representing stages. That distinction was made most profoundly and with the largest impact by Dorothy Sayers' in *The Lost*

Tools of Learning. While I do disagree that these are exclusively stages I find the distinction to be particularly helpful in light of designing good curricula. As such, within this chapter which emphasizes how you, as a teacher, put 21st Century Trivium into practice, I will consider these in the stage form without committing myself to agreeing with it fully. It is, for design purposes that I will leverage it in this way and I am confident that readers will find it helpful.

It is not possible to make proper and sound judgments without a broad base of accurate knowledge. This is why the grammar stage is foundational and primary, and recognized as the first stage of the Trivium. Equally, it is not possible for that base of knowledge to be stable and secure if we do not engage critically with that information. So, in our second stage we employ logic to engage with these topics and learn the rules of the domain. If either of these foundations is weak, a person's rhetorical skill will suffer greatly or perhaps worse, they will become an influential orator who opines on anything and everything but in an utterly vacuous and illusory manner.

In the case of a learner who lacks sufficient and/or accurate knowledge who jumps into expression of thought you get a lot of pontification, unwarranted pride, and strengthened false beliefs within individuals that they know what they are talking about even though nothing could be further from the truth. Such persons literally don't know what they don't know and are perfect illustrations of a true fool. In the case of a learner who has broad and rich knowledge but lacks any critical engagement with it we are left with a passive and shallow learner whose rigid understanding lacks awareness of the beauty of concepts in their full complexity. Both of these cases will lead to circumstances in which learners are engaging in creative and critical expression without having sufficient knowledge and skill to do so. Consequently, both of these must be avoided and we are faced with the benefit of following the trivium's three stages intentionally and fully. The design of the trivium in stages works to our advantage in this way: Knowledge is ensured to precede criticism, application, and contemplation and yet these latter aims are the real aims of learning – it is designed to equip learners with the necessary tools to get there.

The trivium framework as a model for learning also serves as a logical guide for instruction. As such, teachers can reflect on the stage of learning at which they are working[1] and allow that information to determine the most appropriate instructional practices. In general, the transition moves through what is commonly referred to as gradual release. During the grammar phase of learning, the teacher is director of learning, taking lead, providing information, instruction, and correction. What this means in the context of a classroom, is that the teacher is doing most of the leading for learning. And when exploring new ideas this should virtually always be the case. During the logic phase of learning, a shift begins to occur in which teacher and student take on shared accountability for leading learning. In the context of the classroom, this means that while the teacher is still grand designer of learning and continues to instruct, require student practice, and so forth, there is an increasing emphasis on requiring students to step into the roles for leading of learning. They are to interact with material from various perspectives: Comparison, decomposition; asking what if; offering informed criticism; and so forth. Finally, as we shift into the rhetoric phase of learning the transition completes and students are demanded to do more of the leading for learning. This does not mean that at these higher stages that teachers do not instruct; rather, it means that the ratio of time is likely to be reduced because by this point the learners themselves should be equipped with appropriate background knowledge and essential skills that they can learn some when pushed into roles of teaching. Furthermore, they can also be expected to engage in more in-depth lecture that challenges rather than merely instructing. So, the framework is not a clean transition from one to another but more a shift in priority for instruction.

An Overview of the 21st Century Trivium General Teaching Suggestions

One of the great benefits of the trivium approach as being thought of as stages is the way it guides teachers in broadly where the focus of instruction and what the focus of learning ought to be. This structure helps clarify a progression through which learners ought to move as they develop in a domain. While the trivium does not tell you "what" to include at each stage; it does help you focus on those topics that will provide more leverage for later learning and offer a consistent pattern for learning. Through the rest of this chapter we will look at instructional principles and strategies teachers should consider implementing as they lead learners through the trivium and in the next chapter, I will provide specific content and skills you should expect to see in differing content areas to help get you started in your domain and make connections to others.

Considering the model through the three-phase sequence that the trivium provides through its framework offers guidance on types of instructional practice that are more and less appropriate at the various stages. Table 7.1 outlines a summary of this and in what follows I will extend on each of these phases in subsequent sections. I will expand on these phases and their implications for instruction, learning, and assessment and I must note right up front that *just because a pedagogical approach is a priority does not mean it is inappropriate in other phases*. This is a general guideline from which you should consult and begin, but it is not the end to which everything must adhere.

This framework of the trivium is also scalable. That is, within one class you can help students move through the phases of grammar, logic, and rhetoric but that this is also true of the larger domain, as well. In this way, schools

Table 7.1 Trivium Stage and Pedagogical Priority

Category	Grammar Phase	Logic Phase	Rhetoric Phase
Gradual release pattern (generally)	"I do" (teacher)	"We do" (teacher & student)	"You do" (student)
Priority pedagogical practices	• Direct Instruction (More) • Practice, practice, practice • Share concepts • Explain rules • Provide resources • Teach study skills • Ritualize repetition • Provide scaffolding • Explicitly connect ideas • Routinize key processes	• Direct Instruction (Some) • Guided Discovery (With prior knowledge) • Debates • Logic • Questioning • Exploration • Structured Discussion • Model habits of discussion • Provide graphic organizers • Introduce complexity	• Direct Instruction (New) • Formal Debate • Evaluation • Lecture • Demand Eloquent expression • Model self-reflection • Express counterpoints in their best light • Pose open-ended questions • Pose problems • Critiques of the good and beautiful

(Continued)

Table 7.1 Trivium Stage and Pedagogical Priority (Continued)

Category	Grammar Phase	Logic Phase	Rhetoric Phase
Key aim of phase	*Develop a broad knowledge-base*	*Understanding complexities & patterns of knowledge*	*Articulate and defend reasoned positions elegantly & persuasively*
Learner experiences	<ul><li>Memorize content</li><li>Take notes – draw / words</li><li>Access information</li><li>Acquire skills</li><li>Learn to delay critique</li><li>Cultivate wonder and curiosity to learn</li><li>Learn habits</li><li>Enjoy learning</li><li>Creative opportunities</li><li>Admire content – wonder at the content</li></ul>	<ul><li>Explore content</li><li>Connect ideas & concepts</li><li>Compare and contrast diverse information</li><li>Guided practice</li><li>Learn to engage civilly with diverse views</li><li>Learn to accurately represent all views</li><li>Work hard</li><li>Creative application</li><li>Critique content – appreciate content in context</li></ul>	<ul><li>Analyze and evaluate content</li><li>Evaluate ideas</li><li>Collect, organize, and synthesize information</li><li>Embody skills through performance, presentation</li><li>Learn to justify thoughts and reflect on learning</li><li>Learn that learning leads to more questions</li><li>Articulately express views</li><li>Present elegant argument</li><li>Creative expression</li></ul>
Assessments (samples)	Reciting knowledge Repeating information Drawing Short Response	Precis Writing Dialogue: Teacher-Student Argument Map Short Essay	Speech/Presentation Oral Defense Inquiry Project Essay/Thesis

– or homeschoolers – look at the big picture of learning in a domain and determine what degree of emphasis ought to be placed in each phase of the learning process as learners develop.

Learning is gradual and requires that learners reorganize and refine their knowledge. What specific instructional practices should we consider in light of this? First, do not drive by. Linger. You cannot be in a rush to get through "x" so you can move onto "y". Slow it down. Adopt the classical pedagogical principle of *festina lente* – make haste slowly. Model and encourage students to wonder about things, encourage them to ask what if and to consider maybe. Cultivate their curiosity in the subject matter while avoiding distractions so that you do not have to rush.

To promote more effective classroom discussions, put this principle into practice. For instance, precede your discussions with individual silent time for contemplation followed by silent time for individual writing and reflection. Then, engage in discussion. This will not just allow but require learners to slow down, to process information, to contemplate on the idea at hand and it will both focus the discussion and bring learners to the discussion more equipped. Provide time at the conclusion of the discussion to reflect and contemplate on the focus of the discussion and then provide an expert-constructed summary recapping the key take-aways from the discussion. Allow for another round of processing and while we have slowed down our pace, we have helped ensure our learners to not think that you can succeed in "drive-by learning"! We need to slow it down, to intentionally reflect on what we are learning, and do so again and again.

When designing your lessons and units be sure to provide ample opportunities to retrieve information in varied ways such as oral recitation, short quizzes, quick partner shares, and so forth. The idea is to ensure that learners practice retrieving knowledge from their memory in various contexts and spread across time, which leads to stronger and more usable memory traces (Sara, 2000). So, let's now consider some specific examples that we might employ at the stage of grammar, logic, and rhetoric. First, we'll examine the grammar stage whose primary purpose is to develop a broad knowledge base in the learner to draw upon for extended learning tasks as well as cultivate humility in the hard-work it takes to learn well.

Instructional Principles and Grammar

The grammar phase is both essential in providing the necessary foundations and essential to allow learners to experience engaging and entertaining methods that balance out some of the monotony that is required to effectively move through this phase. The first priority – necessary foundations – is primary but one should not discount the role of this second priority – engaging and entertaining opportunities. A grammar phase without consideration of this first priority is no grammar phase at all. A grammar phase that fails to consider the second priority, however, could result in an educational environment that fails to equip learners for the next phases. In order for learners to be ready to recognize the nuances and complexity of our constant pursuit of knowledge they must recognize that they won't always get everything right. They must also recognize that learning is a process and that as they encounter more knowledge, it will likely lead to more nuance and more awareness of one's own ignorance. In these encounters, a child whose experiences have not considered the second priorities is likely to hit a wall in which they lose interest or lack confidence and competence to explore further in ways that will only heighten one's awareness of what they do not know.

Spatial relationships help us see structures. Additionally, you begin to search for relationships across the different pieces of information. At the grammar stage, one of best strategies to employ is to provide learners with teacher constructed graphic organizers that the students fill in during a lesson. In this way, the structure is provided to them by the expert who saw it all along, and at the end, they have a strong visual that organizes key information. Figure 7.1 shows two examples of a concept map including notes as to where the teacher should preset information and where the student should add their own.

Guided Concept Organizer

Write the term here

Write a teacher-provided definition (book, e.g.)

Write a simple definition in your own words

Teacher-provided visual example

Teacher-provided visual example

Connections | Questions

Examples

Student-generated visual example

Student-generated visual example

Non-Examples

Figure 7.1 Concept map templates.

Figure 7.2 A Book of Excellence in History cover page.

Virtually every student will be a novice in virtually every circumstance but through more and intentional exposure to knowledge they move on a pathway towards expertise. In light of this reality, how can instruction promote this progression? First off, display work of experts and revere it for its beauty, its precision, and make explicit the steadfast, not hurried, work that went into getting there. You might consider developing a book of excellence for your area in which students copy the work of the masters and also have opportunities for their own creations. This deliberate juxtaposition is a great way to provide them a sense of what excellence looks like and allows for them to attempt to mirror its elegance and precision. Figure 7.2 provides a sample of a book of excellence I required students to create from a history course for high school students.

Later on I would have students revisit this "Book of Excellence" and interact with it again when engaging in the logic and rhetoric stages of their learning experience in my classroom. I'll note examples of what that looked like later. And by taking this slow approach that makes it important to understand the work of masters first, we cultivate in our students a respect of expertise and the hard work it takes to achieve it. We impart a love for the pursuit of truth, goodness and beauty that acknowledges the long duration of deliberately challenging oneself and getting feedback from more knowledge persons to get there. In this way we can help instill in our learners an understanding that it is okay that we are not experts; expertise takes a great deal of time.

One additional strategy you could employ here is what I refer to as "The Ballpark". Simply put we task our students with putting a key word/concept/topic/central idea at the center of a page of paper or a white board and then, they first write down as many topics, concepts, persons, and so forth that they think may connect to that central idea. Giving them just a minute or so to do this is helpful in two ways: (1) It helps them and you recognize the breadth of the background knowledge they see connected to the topic at hand, and (2) by casting this wide net it might cue them into things that were not the first to come to their mind but that may be relevant. My colleague and I use this a lot with our doctoral students when planning a research study but it can be used incredibly effectively as a quick form of low-stakes retrieval practice and point you, as the teacher, to potential misconceptions or affirm that the group is ready to move forward. Figure 7.3 provides an example of a completed "Ballpark" activity.

This is what a great deal of the grammar stages is all about: Building knowledge and cultivating humility about the time it takes to learn things well. As we progress we will equip our learners with a broad foundation of knowledge so that their working memory is less strained when we get ready

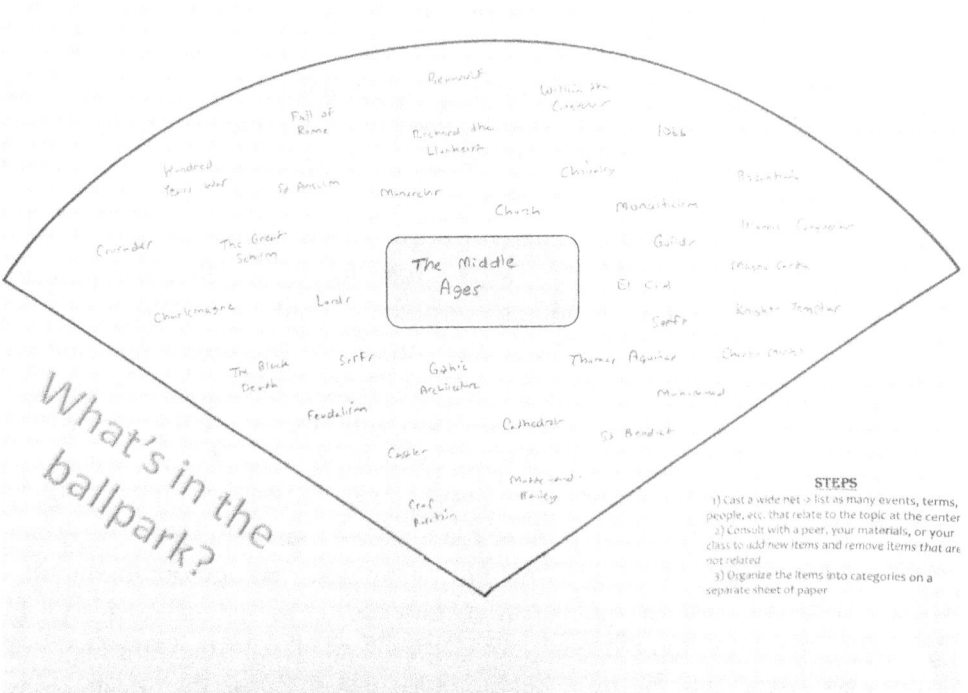

Figure 7.3 What's in the Ballpark? Activity to check prior knowledge.

to shift our emphasis towards more logical and rhetorical exercises. So, in our progression through the trivium we will now turn to the logic stage with the aim of employing strategies that will help learners understand complexities and patterns of knowledge.

Instructional Principles and Logic

One thing to keep in mind is that throughout all these stages we ought to engage in consistent practice because that practice will challenge our learners to retrieve key information, connect it with other topics, and build richer and stronger connections that endure much more effectively. In that regard, within the logic phase it would be wise to ask lots of questions. Probe and expand on essential knowledge. Challenge students to paraphrase what others have said and confirm the paraphrase is right to highlight the importance of accuracy and precision. Compare examples, challenge students to break them down into specific distinctions of what makes them similar and different.

Take advantage of the *testing effect* by employing low-stakes quizzes frequently in your classroom. The testing effect occurs as learning is enhanced by taking tests and receiving corrective and actionable feedback (Smith, Roediger, & Karpicke, 2013). You could do that by giving quizzes distributed across the learning in various forms each followed by self-assessment and corrections. For example, you could develop weekly flash cards for studying and employ spaced practice in a "Now-Recent-Past Flash Card Review" every week. Perhaps you identify three to five essential things to master each week and have students spend just a few minutes each Friday building those flash cards. This review strategy is a way to help them see the need for review never goes away but becomes less frequent as we continue to grow in understanding of information. As your students' stacks of flash cards grow, they start to move them into one of the following categories: Now (this month), Recent (this past month), and Past (the entire year – anything longer than a month ago). New cards are placed on the bottom of a stack. At least during the next week, allocate six minutes for "Recent-Past Flash Card" review. They should spend three minutes reviewing cards in the "Now" pile, two minutes reviewing cards in the "Recent" pile, and one minute reviewing cards in the "Past" pile. At the start of each month, shuffle the cards up in every deck as well so that the sequence is not predictable – this will help make the retrieval more effective. And here's another pro tip (I know because I failed to do my first time and organizing this was difficult, ha-ha): You might consider color coding these flash cards to help students figure out when they can move to the next stack! An example of this strategy is illustrated in Figure 7.4 – students can keep this in their desk if they

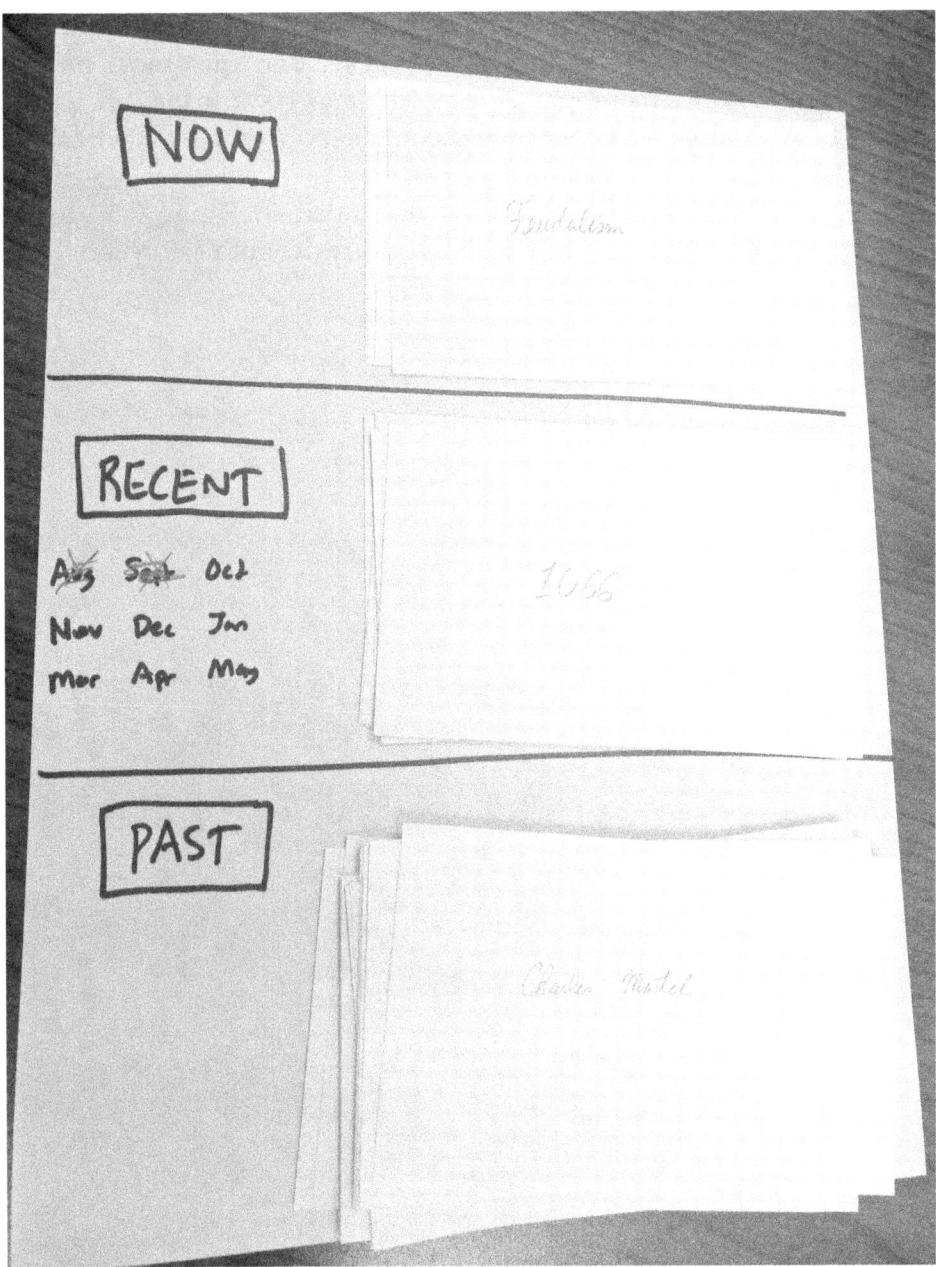

Figure 7.4 Now-recent-past review strategy.

have an old fashioned one with a cubby in it, or you can place them into plastic bags labeled and it will accomplish the exact same thing.

As the year goes on you might consider adjusting this to a two–two–two minute split as the "past" deck gets much larger than the others as you can imagine! In this way, you'll constantly be employing spaced, retrieval practice for your students and help them see that we don't just move on from things and never touch them again. We revisit them, because they are important and the more time we linger with them, the more time they will stick in our minds!

A "Mind Material Partner" review illustrated in Figure 7.5[2]. In this activity you would open up class with a short review of past material with

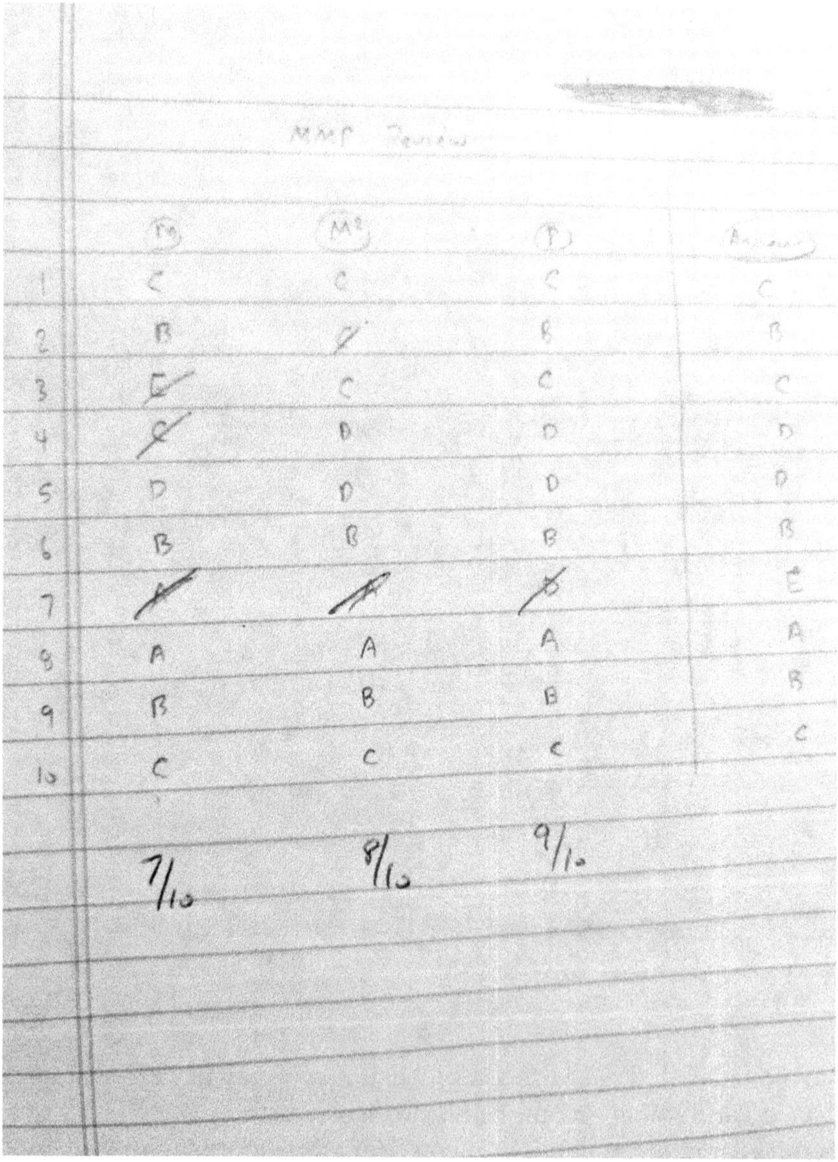

Figure 7.5 Mind Material Partner for retrieval practice.

selected response and/or short answer questions. First, give individuals a few minutes to attempt to answer all items simply from memory (M – Mind). Next, give them a few minutes to review their materials and see if they would change any responses (M – Material). Finally, give them a few minutes to discuss with a partner and make adjustments (P – Partner). I would, then, reveal the answer key to them and encourage them to record it along with keeping all the material.

Grading such practice assessments does not help the learner grow but, interestingly, correcting the work after receiving feedback does. Engage your learners in this purposeful form of practice. Consistent application of practice in the key skills and of the essential knowledge to be learned is one of the best ways to promote learning that lasts. Every time a memory is brought to mind it is not just seen again but it is reconstructed and reinforced and so practicing is not just about checking our memory but about enhancing it.

Since an emphasis of learning in the logic phase is metacognitive – or thinking about thinking – it is wise to make that explicit for your students. To help students move gradually through logical engagement with your discipline, consider having them build upon their grammar-stage developed "Book of Excellence" that captured high quality work of experts in the field curated by the teacher. Now, intersperse that book with student opportunities to draw upon the work of the masters to create their own attempts at progressing in their skills. Say, for instance, that we had them copy down a critique by eminent historians of a poorly developed historical project[3]. By studying how top historians critique the work of others students can start to see patterns in what is looked for – in other words, they see examples of the rules of a domain (in history in this example) are applied by top experts in the field. After having studied some examples such as this, the students would try their hand at critiquing student-developed historical essays applying the same skills.

One final illustration of an instructional approach you could consider to develop logical competence in your subject area would be to challenge students to compose syllogisms. A syllogism is a series of statements that lead to a conclusion[4]. Have students break down arguments about topics into syllogisms following the pattern of P implies Q, P, therefore Q. Here is what that actually looks like:

- P -> Q   [If it is raining outside the ground is wet]
- P   [It is raining outside]
- Q   [Therefore, the ground is wet]

Breaking positions down into this form of reasoning is really helpful as it often points us to errors in reasoning. Furthermore, it makes us break down long claims to simpler to interact with statements. And once we have done so, we can check to see if we have good reasons and evidence to believe the statements or if there are good reasons and evidence to believe their negation. Either way, composing syllogisms is another great strategy to help your students examine the rules of reasoning in context.

Now we will shift our attention to the last stage of the trivium: Rhetoric. In the rhetoric stage, our primary aim is to train students to be able to articulate and defend reasoned, evidence-informed, positions that are stated elegantly, persuasively, and coherently.

Instructional Principles and Rhetoric

At the latter stages of learning in our class we want to move students towards increased engagement in application, creation, expression, and so forth. This is what we consider the rhetoric stage in this framework. If we have followed these stages so far we have likely developed a strong foundation of knowledge and humility in our students. We have likely helped them to examine developments in the domain and engage with controversies developing a longer view so they are less likely to jump to conclusions. And with those competencies in tow they are ready to move into the phases where we challenge them to articulate their own understanding and positions on relevant topics to the domain. Our learners are now in the position of the wise man as Aristotle saw him: Those who speak not because they have to but, rather, because they have something to say.

Here are a few strategies you should have students employ as they develop their rhetorical skill in your area. The first relates to what I did in the opening two chapters in this book: Create maxims for key ideas. Maxims – or axioms/principles – are basic statements that sum up general truths. As such, they provide some helpful guidance for interacting with a domain. Table 7.2 outlines three specific types of maxims you can challenge your students to create along with examples provided for each.

Another great strategy for developing the rhetorical skill of students is to engage them in competing ideas with an emphasis on presenting the best case for *both sides*. Often, we stop at making the best case for our own side but consider taking this a step further to help your learners demonstrate their depth of understanding of competing views and move closer to wisdom. Some strategies to help you in that regard including having students develop a confirmation and refutation table for a topic. An example of this is provided in Table 7.3.

Table 7.2 Maxims to Develop Rhetorical Skill

Type of Maxim	Description	Example
Analogical Maxim	Inventing an analogy to help illustrate an important truth	Reveal the playbook to your students like a coach reveals the playbook to his or her team
Personal Maxim	Explaining a proverb, maxim, or principle in your own words	Take one of the six principles of learning I have shared and reword it in your own language
Reversed Maxim	Explaining what will happen if a proverb, maxim, or principle is not heeded to form a new maxim	By failing to show your learners their plan for learning you fail to prepare them for success

A refutation table like this provides an outline for engaging with persons whom we may not disagree but in a fashion that is eloquent and prudent as opposed to one that is more confrontational. It also presents a carefully sequenced set of steps to organize a response that both confirms a position, as well as another that refutes it. This helps the learner see nuances in the controversy and develop a compassion that those who never try to understand both sides do not develop.

Table 7.3 Confirmation and Refutation

Confirmation	Refutation
1. Praise the good reputation of the proponent
2. Explain – or narrate – the matter
3. Point out the merits of the argument
4. Demonstrate how many have been convinced
5. Prove the position as entirely probable by showing it is consistent, proper, and reasonable in light of the evidence	1. State the false assertion made by the proponent as accurately as possible
2. Explain – or narrate – the matter
3. Show the obscurity of the opposition
4. Articulate the erroneous aspects of the opposing view
5. Show the improbability of the position to show it is inconsistent, irrational, and/or not reasonable in light of the evidence

The rhetoric stage for learners is aimed at equipping them to communicate effectively and accurately about a domain. This moves beyond focusing on what they prefer or their opinion but rather, their capacity to articulate competing views on relevant topics in the domain accurately. Employing the strategies presented herein will help you engage learners towards the end of their experience to develop this ability and prepare them to be more prudent and wiser.

Classical Pedagogy for Understanding

An education that utilizes the trivium and the classical approach will typically utilize a series of pedagogical principles. Dr. Christopher Perrin is the publisher of *Classical Academic Press* and is an advocate for classical education. In his work, he articulates eight essential principles of classical pedagogy: (1) Festinal lente (make haste slowly); (2) multum non multa (much not many); (3) repetitio mater memoriae (repetition, the mother of memory); (4) songs and chants; (5) embodied education; (6) educational virtues; (7) wonder and curiosity; and (8) schole and contemplation[5]. I have seen two other suggested principles for classical education as well: (9) Docendo discimus and (10) optimus magister liber bonus est.

Within this section, I want to classify these pedagogical principles into my own systematically constructed domains of understanding, which are derived from the best evidence available with regards to cognition. Table 7.4 provides a juxtaposition of my principles – and a brief overview of each – and which of these classical pedagogical principles fit within each.

The essential principles of understanding relate to ways through which the trivium improves learning and understanding for students. Furthermore, I will use Dr. Christopher Perrin's classical pedagogical principles within each as a means to explicitly bridge between the old (classical) and the new (cognitive science) and thus present an integrated approach to implementing this framework in your setting. To begin let us start with the most fundamental principle we want to think about as educators: We design the environments our students engage in. There is no excuse for an ill-structured or chaotic environment unless we want to leave success to chance. So, before thinking about how to cultivate understanding take a minute to reflect on the most basic, first step: Order. Establish a well-ordered educational environment. Human beings thrive on routines. Be sure that in your classroom, students learn and abide by your chosen routines – ones that promote habits that will tip learners towards both end goals and that provide consistency and order for students in a chaotic world.

Table 7.4 Pedagogical Principles for a Trivium Focused Path to Understanding

Essential Principle of Understanding	Brief Overview	Embedded Classical Pedagogical Principles
Understanding is not Accidental	There are progressions to learning and aims for learning. A learning environment can be designed so that understanding is not accidental.	• Festina Lente • Repetitio Mater Memoriae • Docendo Discimus
Understanding precedes Application	Before diving into application, it is essential that learners have an accurate understanding of what they are trying to apply.	• Multum non Multa • Schole/ Contemplation
Understanding is enhanced through meaning	Learning is enhanced when it is meaningful and when creative expression is allowed after knowledge is in place	• Embodied Education • Schole/ Contemplation
Understanding can be enriched through creativity	After students have adequate knowledge in place allowing for creative expression enriches learning	• Wonder & Curiosity • Optimus Magister Liber Bonus Est

Understanding Is Not Accidental

Constantly facing decisions in the moment is an inevitable element of teaching – a job that changes, literally by the second. But when it comes to students and their developing understanding of our material we need to ensure our organizational approaches tip them towards understanding by design. That is why we began by placing importance on an ordered educational environment. And it helps because if your aim is to be effective for all your students, understanding is too important to leave to chance. True understanding requires extended thought, it rests on knowledge, and it reflects and considers how something might be applied. Consequently, as educators we must work to build an environment in which understanding does not occur by accident, but as the result of interacting with our well-designed learning environment. The foundation of that environment is order. Once we reflect on and ensure that we build an environment tipped towards order that will promote effective learning we then move towards choosing the right tools and strategies to promote understanding.

I will emphasize five specific organizational strategies that any educator can employ and use in his or her context to improve student understanding and learning[6]. First off, when mapping out your curriculum you should think about the big picture and design your curriculum as an investigation into significant, deep, and explanatory questions relevant to the content area. The structure of using such questions helps enhance understanding while promoting a long view of the learner and a readiness to accept the classical motto of *festina lente* – in English, to make haste, slowly. We know our aim – to answer this question – but to do so we recognize it will take time. We cannot dive into the deep end to answer; rather we must linger in the shallows to get immersed as we steadily move towards our attempt to answer the question. Through using these deep explanatory questions, we can encourage our students to address deep level questions on relevant course material as a consistent aim for each instructional unit. In this way, an educator takes the long aim for each unit by guiding the development of a deep explanatory question and promotes a commitment to make haste, slowly. There is not a rush to get to the end but rather a steadfast progress towards that end.

The remaining four organizational strategies all align neatly with the classical pedagogical principle of *repetitio mater memoriae* – in English, that repetition is the mother of memory. When it comes to classical pedagogical approaches a consistent diet of repetition is recognized as essential to making the learning your own. Research from cognitive science bears out this claim very strongly, so let's look at four specific organizational strategies that we can employ to maximize the effectiveness of such practice.

The next organizational strategy that should be adopted to not leave understanding to chance is that when students are being introduced to new material it should combine graphics with verbal descriptions. It is important that any text descriptions appear near the related visual representations to ensure the strongest positive impact on student understanding. Interestingly, studies have consistently found that students learn more when the verbal description is presented in audio form (or read) as opposed to being presented as written text[7]. To integrate this, the effective pedagogical approach is that when you are teaching students about processes and procedures that can be represented meaningfully through pictures, figures, charts, and other graphic formats, it is wise to combine verbal descriptions of the process with graphical representations that illustrate those steps.

Furthermore, in order to not leave understanding to luck, an effective educator should mix up how students complete their work. This is referred to as *interleaved* practice and was discussed earlier in Chapter Two. Basically, the ideal approach to using interleaved practice includes two distinct and yet similar approaches. First, rather than giving students a set of twenty questions to complete on their own, understanding is better achieved when a variety of worked examples[8] are mixed in (not added on top of) those questions. That is, a student who views one worked example, followed by four problems they must solve themselves, followed by another worked example, and four more student-completed solutions, continuing until the same number of items (20) is completed will learn better. This leverages the benefits of worked examples in conjunction with the benefits of interleaving – an approach that changes the type of question or task to be completed at each point. So, another approach to interleave your students work is to mix up the types of practice so that an assignment consisting of those 20 items might include three or four different types of questions rather than simply doing the same exact type each time. What happens when you do this is that you are forced to dig back into your memory again and again to decide what each type of question is asking rather than simply doing all twenty the exact same way. This approach can seem more challenging for learners but the mixing up of repeated practice leads to richer learning and understanding, which is why these strategies are called *desirable difficulties*.

I have constructed Figure 7.6 as a visual summary of these key organizational principles that effective educators should put into practice to ensure that understanding happens by design and not just on accident.

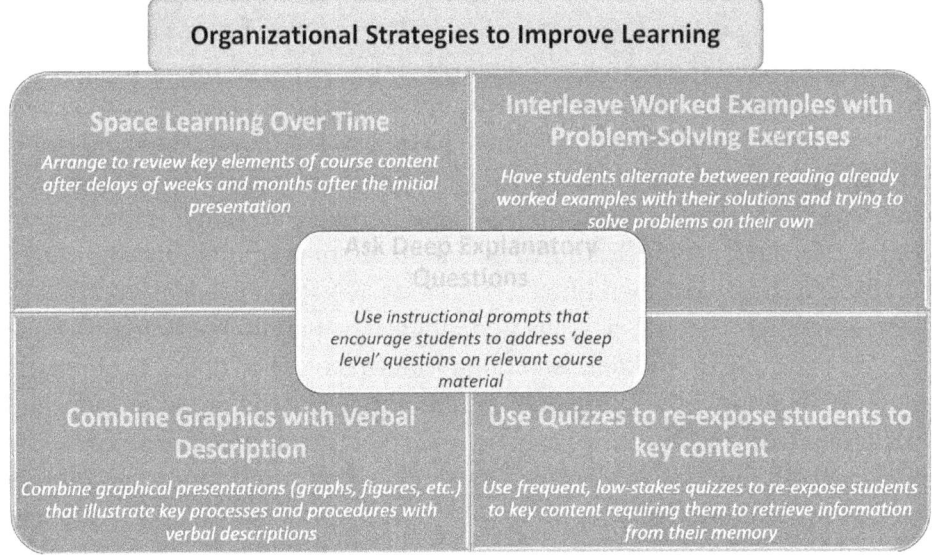

Figure 7.6 Organizational strategies to enhance learning.

Finally, the classical pedagogical principal of *docendo discumus* aligns very well with the principle that understanding is not accidental. An effective teacher understands his or her subject and is able to utilize the art of teaching informed by science of learning to build coherent learning experiences that lead to understanding *by design*. Most of us who have taught something have experienced this reality – that in trying to design a learning experience – or experiences – that will lead to learning we had to first spend a great deal more time learning the material than we did before. This is how *docendo discumus* comes into play. Assigning your child to *teach* material they do not understand yet is not what we are calling for in this. Instead, as students move towards mastery in a domain challenging them to teach it to others is a way to make them improve their learning even more. The wise educator will not overdo assigning teaching to his or her students because, yes, it will enhance their learning, but it takes far more time than letting the master direct the learning. Choose wisely the opportunities to allow learners to leverage this and equip them with an appreciation of the challenge involved in teaching for understanding.

Understanding Precedes Application and Is Enhanced Through Meaning

In the world in which we live almost everyone is always in a rush to get to applying things. While our aim is to help learners so that they can apply them – considering the role that understanding plays in effective application is important. As such, we want to help our learners thrive by building up their knowledge-base and understanding to a sufficient level *before* diving into application. In order to address this important fact, we should draw on the classical pedagogical principle of *Festina lente* – to make haste, slow down. In other words, avoid the rush to doing; especially when dealing with students who have limited prior knowledge in an area where you may have them "do". As I have noted before, we make haste towards understanding not by "driving by" in learning but by slowing down. Understanding requires sustained and focused concentration. As such, perhaps the single most important thing we can do for meaningful development of student understanding is to give them the time they require.

Several others of these classical pedagogical principles speak to this factor. First, the principle of *multum non multa*. In terms of developing understanding we are dealing with diving deeper into topics. So, the broad foundations, while crucial, are not the emphasis here. Rather, when it comes to exploring topics in depth the wise teacher will carefully select important topics in their domain to give these deep explorations rather than trying to do so on everything. Additionally, the principle of *embodied education* places emphasis on the fact that we, humans, are not just information processing machines. We are endowed with senses beyond that, and, that because of that there is meaningful opportunity to enhance learning by tapping into the broader senses. Once students have developed reasonable knowledge about something, give them opportunities to experience it that will tap into our other senses – smell, taste, touch, and so forth. Leverage our experience to enhance understanding once basic understanding is in place.

One final classical pedagogical strategy that is particularly helpful in regards to enhancing understanding through meaning and ensuring understanding precedes application is through *schole*[9]. Schole comes from the Greek word for leisure, which also happens to be the origin of the Latin word for school. The name for institutions of learning means leisure[10]. Schole is really about focusing deeply on the first principle of learning that I shared: Learning takes time and contemplation. As such it places an emphasis on losing oneself in the pursuit of truth; thinking about the meaning of things and implications of that beyond just knowing it; reflecting on what it means for what is good and beautiful, and so forth. In a word, schole is about contemplation – and contemplation ought to occur to help develop our understanding better so that when we are ready to dive into application, we have interacted with the tensions of rest and rigor. So, understanding ought to precede our application and it also is enhanced when we examine concepts in a contemplative and reflective manner seeking to see their meaning. We can also leverage creativity as a means to enrich understanding.

Understanding Can Be Enriched Through Creativity

Creativity generally encompasses three components: Novelty, usefulness, and context. That is, creativity takes place when someone makes something that is new, productive, and bound to a particular domain. This does not have to be on the scale of the discovery of a new mathematical formula to explain the working of the universe such as Einstein's famous $e=mc^2$, but is scalable. For instance, most of what our students will do creativity will not be generating any new knowledge but rather refashioning knowledge in a context that is interesting and novel to them. This everyday type of creativity is referred to as *little c creativity* as opposed to revolutionary innovations or creations such as Einstein's formula, which is referred to as *big c creativity*. Teresa Amabile, an eminent creativity researcher describes this distinction by contrasting the invention of the paperclip as an example of *big c creativity* while every time someone comes up with a new use for it that is meaningful to them it is *little c creativity*. We ought not to expect our students to do a lot of *big c creativity* because they will, in the overwhelming amount of cases, lack the expertise to do so. However, cultivating *little c creativity* allows for meaningful expansion of their learning in that doing so enriches their understanding. Let's look at a few examples of specific types of creative expression we can cultivate in our classroom to promote creative thinking and deepening our learners' understanding.

One of the most powerful expressions of creativity comes through the development of analogies. To draw an analogy requires that one finds underlying similarity between diverse instances. As such, analogical reasoning is a powerful way to learn new concepts and principles. It is, in fact, a common practice used by experts in their field to explain novel ideas. Johannes Kepler, who developed the concept of gravity to explain planetary orbits through this approach "worked out his theory of gravity by drawing an analogy to the rays of the sun. The rays of the sun become weaker at a distance, so by analogy, gravity does too" (Schwartz, Tsang, & Blair (2016), p. 3).

When people examine multiple things, however, they tend to be distracted by shared surface features, which are those readily perceived properties. The aim for deeper understanding is towards focusing in on connections and that requires looking to the deep structure, or relations among elements. The key for using analogies to enhance learning is in finding the common principle despite the surface differences. A wonderful example of this is when people say that all religions are the same. Those who make such a claim are looking at the surface features – they seem to follow some similar practices, have similar commitments and codes, and so forth. However, once you examine the deep structure or relations among religions we find that they are superficially the same but that they are fundamentally different. They differ on the important questions at the heart of the practice and simply share rituals, for instance. How can instruction and student understanding be enhanced through use of analogies?

- Explain new ideas by making good analogies to familiar ideas

By using analogies for new ideas with ideas we are familiar with we build additional pathways within our webs of understanding. This entrenches new learning with already familiar material and allows for learning to both endure and to be more easily understood.

- Provide learners with multiple examples and ask them to find the underlying structure

Having students find analogous structure among different items is a very powerful approach to enhancing student understanding. This is particularly powerful in that it exposes learners to a range of variation that might appear for a particular principle. So, interacting with multiple examples and looking for what is similar at a deeper level will lead to more enduring and better understanding.

Additionally, the most obvious connection to enriching understanding through creativity to the classical pedagogical principle of *wonder and curiosity*. Through engaging the interest of learners we can enhance their understanding. You could look back in Chapter Six where I presented some specific strategies that linked to creativity and wonder. This does not mean that they should pursue whatever they want as often they do not know what they need (Kirschner & Van Merrienboer, 2013), however, it would be equally foolish to stamp out their interests and fail to engage with them in a walk alongside the learners rather than a march to which they follow your every step without question. Challenging learners to think deeply and employ productive creativity related to a topic requires them to think at high levels and promotes deeper understanding. And we might also leverage the great works of incredible writers of the past by applying the classical pedagogical principle of *optimus magister liber bonus est*, which is just Latin for "the best teacher is a good book". No matter what subject you are teaching look for classic works, and current ones, that are widely recognized for their eloquence and for teaching concepts relevant for your class. This principle affirms the great underlying belief of liberal education that humanity has long been engaged in a great conversation and we ought to invite our students to become part of that great conversation, sooner, rather than later.

In promoting a deeper understanding of material for our learners one of the best approaches is to create an environment in which they are not simply permitted to be creative (passive and left to chance) but one in which they are promoted to engage in creative expression by design. An astute reader may have noted, however, that nowhere have I currently addressed the classical principle of *docendo discimus*. This was intentional because that principle is aligned to a consideration of all four of these principles of learning. *Docendo discimus*, which translated from Latin into English means "by teaching we learn", is an especially powerful pedagogical practice to employ. However, depending on the extent to which each of these four aspects are considered it will be rendered more or less effective. And its alignment to all of these principles of understanding allows for the benefit of saving the best for last because it is perhaps the single best way to enhance understanding and yet requires substantial efforts before doing so and will likely be the last to employ with your learners.

In order for someone to effectively teach something it presumes that they are not simply working by luck. That is, that they understand because they have put the hard effort into learning the idea and that through teaching well they are compelled to apply all of these principles. One can teach quite poorly, however, if these four principles of understanding all are adequately met, that is highly unlikely. In order to teach well, we must have an understanding of what we are trying to teach. We must see the progressions through learning and intentionally cultivate an environment that will lead learners towards understanding. Teaching is an application and, as such, recognizes that I must put in the hard work before diving into teaching to ensure that understanding is achieved before I direct others as to where to go. Teaching forces one to examine critically what things mean, why they matter, who should care, and so forth, each of which necessitates a consideration of meaning. Consequently, the teacher must think deliberately about meaning and attempt to get the learners to engage with that as well. Finally, in order for someone to design an instructional sequence it demands a great deal of creativity. And so the principle of *docendo discimus* is a wonderful capstone type of experience for learners through which they can demonstrate understanding in a way that is by design, requires knowledge and skills to be in place, focuses in on meaning, and demands creative expression. What a powerful culmination for enhancing understanding through a classical pedagogical lens!

Summary

In this chapter we have surveyed four essential commitments to principled application of instructional approaches, revisited our basic axioms/principles of learning and offered specific illustrations of what they look like, outlined a basic progression model of instructional approaches, and wrapped up with how applying basic classical pedagogical strategies can be leveraged to enhance understanding in our learners. Next we will consider specific content areas, essentials to consider, and then wrap up our look at making learning intentional through the systematic application of the trivium, as informed by cognitive science.

For Reflection and Application

Thinking back on this chapter, consider the following reflective tasks and ideas for application in your classroom:

1 Review the various instructional ideas in this chapter for the grammar stage and choose one that you can adapt for your context right now.

2. Review the various instructional ideas in this chapter for the logic stage and choose one that you can adapt for your context right now.
3. Review the various instructional ideas in this chapter for the rhetoric stage and choose one that you can adapt for your context right now.
4. Consider the principles of classical pedagogy as articulated by Dr. Perrin; which do you think you should to utilize more in your classroom?

Notes

1. Remember that while these are often associated with *ages* they are NOT actually tied to ages but to cognitive development. If you take the trivium model and apply it to any domain your learners could be of any age and *most* pedagogical practices I provide here would be appropriate or could be used with slight modification.
2. I came across this strategy on Twitter but cannot locate whom it originated from so I will plug him anonymously here and he can claim it for a, hopeful, Second Edition.
3. Here is a link to an interview with James McPherson critiquing the 1619 project that students could look at for how top historians critique the work of other historians: https://www.wsws.org/en/articles/2019/11/14/mcph-n14.html.
4. I used syllogisms when interacting with nonsense in education earlier in this book for some examples. Additionally, I would like to note that I am presenting this simply; if you would like to understand more about syllogisms, deductive reasoning, and logic I encourage you to look at Norm Geisler's *Come, let us reason*.
5. An online link with a seminar led by Dr. Perrin is available here in which he lays these principles out: http://insideclassicaled.com/the-eight-essential-principles-of-classical-pedagogy/.
6. In addition to my assertion that these strategies pass the test of cognitive science and classical pedagogical practice, here is a link to a *What Works Clearinghouse* summary that investigated various strategies to improve student learning related to study habits: https://ies.ed.gov/ncee/wwc/Docs/PracticeGuide/20072004.pdf. All five I am emphasizing herein have moderate to strong evidence in favor of their effectiveness. If you follow the link, you'll notice there are others, too, however, I have left them off my list because the preponderance of evidence does not support them at this time.

7. Clark & Mayer, 2003; Clark, 2001; & Mousavi, Low, & Sweller, (1995).
8. A worked example generally is a problem completed by an expert showing the work – the amount of guidance and annotation may vary depending on the level of the student (labeling groups of steps can be particularly helpful for new learners while simply showing the work without the instructional explanation of the steps may be more effective for advanced students)
9. Pronounced SCO – LAY – in case you are wondering ☺
10. Pieper, J. (2009). *Leisure: The basis of culture*, with forward from James Schall. San Francisco, CA: Ignatius Press.

8

Application in Specific Content Areas

Domains of knowledge are taught through the understanding of structures, rules, and precepts of any given domain. Knowledge of these structures, rules, and precepts forms the basis of our collective wisdom in any domain. By applying the grammar and logic stages to a domain, it requires that you focus first and foremost on understanding the essential knowledge (structures) and guiding rules and precepts of a given domain (skills/practices). Equally, we must ensure that during the learning experience in each domain that we do not inculcate a passive sense of blind acceptance. We need to take in this rich knowledge base while still allowing questioning and furthermore, encouraging learners to imagine possibilities, to ask questions, and to leverage those to help them master the essentials while still cultivating a sense of wonder. Moving through the learning sequence in a domain will allow a learner to be equipped with the tools necessary to engage in rhetoric effectively by both acknowledging and engaging with the best ideas of each domain accurately, critically, and intelligently.

History

History is listed first because it ranks among the most important disciplines through which an educated person must be acquainted. The study of history is important in several aspects: (1) It is the single best account we have for the experiences of mankind and our interactions – positive/negative – and our only laboratory for the testing of ideas; (2) it is a frame of reference from which we understand ourselves; (3) it is an essential component for development of our cultural competence or our cultural literacy; and (4) it contextualizes everything else. When one studies scientific advances or literature devoid of the historical context in which they occurred, they miss important details concerning what or why it was developed. History is the focal point through which all human knowledge is contextualized and thus is a critical domain for learning. What essentials would provide a framework for history in the 21st Century Trivium? Here is a list of some:

- Grammar Stage
  - A General Chronology of Human History (from earliest times through 30 years into the past, roughly, including more current events is okay but it is not so much *history* as it is *current affairs* – history requires some passage of time for the currency of emotion to allow the larger picture to settle in)
  - Stories from the Past to Contextualize Major Events
  - Stories from the Past to provoke wonder and curiosity about important historical figures
  - Understand how history and the past are related, and yet distinct
  - Use *Now and Then* activities to cultivate interest in how life was similar/different in the past from the present prioritizing historical empathy (understanding people of the past in *their* context; not ours)
  - Recognize historical artifacts and primary sources as traces from the past that can be analyzed to discover and construct history
- Logic Stage
  - Document Analysis and Interpretation
  - Compare and contrast alternative accounts of the same historical event
  - Recognize that history is fundamentally different from the "telephone game"
  - Critique historical accounts from the past that are skewed politically
  - Understand the critical importance of interpreting historical events in their historical context (developing empathy with the past and its context)
- Rhetoric Stage
  - Build historical arguments and defend them against criticism
  - Evaluate and critique historical analyses from particular vantage points (weighing their contributions, their limitations, etc.

A final point to note with regards to history is that there are diverse domains within history to which this model would apply equally. That is, when studying *medieval history*, a wise learner would be happy to have the general chronology overall but would enhance his or her ability to learn in that domain by first building a richer chronology specific to that time period. The same would be applicable to other domains. So, for those of us who live in areas that are best understood as parts of *Western Civilization* that fact should prioritize the essential topics for our general chronology. For those of us living in other parts of the world, the general chronology should include the important elements from Western Civilization to the rest of the world but also include more relevant and important continental/regional events. As with many of these domains, there is some flexibility but selection of what to include in this general chronological framework must be:

1. **Significance** (large-scale emphasized always over small-scale; that is, an event that has ramifications across the world is to be prioritized over local events that are, in effect, minutiae)
2. **Endurance** (events included on a well-designed timeline will have passed the test of time – that is, they are not recent additions to fit a preferred group's perspective – they are events that have endured as worthy of inclusion over time)
3. **Leverage** (events included on a well-designed timeline will have leverage to the understanding of other historical details; in this way they provide leverage to richer historical competence)

It has been said before – astutely – that he who does not know the past knows nothing; he is a leaf who does not even know it is part of a tree. Consequently, history should *never* be on the chopping block in designing a curriculum. Rather, history must be the backbone of your curriculum, for without it you implicitly promote a narcissistic outlook in your students where the only things that matter to them become their personal opinion and imagination of things rather than recognizing the important step of contextualizing information.

Geography

Typically, geography ought to be completed directly alongside and within the study of history. This different – and yet connected – discipline is another essential piece for developing in learners a sense of the primacy of context. Where events occur, and do not occur, where ideas flourish, or do not flourish, where ideas spread, are all systematically related to both history and geography. As such, these two *social studies* are crucial elements to include as central features of your curriculum. What are some of the important geographical elements to include in the 21st Century Trivium? Here is another starter list:

- Grammar Stage
  - Ability to identify all continents, oceans, and major geographical features (major lakes, seas, mountain ranges, rivers, etc.) of earth
  - Ability to identify most significant political features of one's own country
  - Ability to identify major international political features (to help you with what is worth learning, use the criteria outlined for a good timeline in the history section above)
  - Familiarity with globes and maps and how they are related/distinct
- Logic Stage
  - Recognition that creation of non-physical maps includes interpretive elements by the creator
  - Compare and contrast diverse types of maps from the same location
  - Understand how ideas, cultural patterns, and so on spread geographically and be able to represent this on a map (diffusion)
  - Identify the ways in which physical environment both shapes human societies and is shaped by human interaction
  - Debate proposals for adapting/modifying the physical environment
- Rhetoric Stage
  - Evaluate and critique the merit of particular geographic representations (weighing their contributions, their limitations, etc.)
  - Creating maps for specific purposes and utilizing them to persuade others
  - Develop a large-scale geographic project of an historical era or a political region using various types of maps

Civics

Civics is the study of citizenship. As such, it engages learners in understanding the rights and duties of citizenship, introduces them to civil disagreement over political issues, and immerses them in an experience that will prepare them for their future civic engagement. As such, this discipline is an essential piece for any curriculum and preparing learners to be productive and proactive members of society. A final and important aspect of a good civic curriculum will include explicit opportunities to engage with political disagreement in a civil manner and in a way that prioritizes *accurately understanding* diverse views rather than compelling agreement with particular views. A starter list outlining key aspects of your civics curriculum includes:

- Grammar Stage
  - Understanding roles and responsibilities of individuals and authorities in a republic
  - Distinguish between constitutional powers granted to various branches and levels of government (executive, legislative, judicial; federal, state; etc.)
  - Explain the formation of the United States government (or your home country, if you are not in the USA)
  - Describe how laws are developed and passed
  - Explain how citizens can engage in civic conversation
- Logic Stage
  - Compare and contrast alternative structures for government
  - Explain how laws are implemented and interpreted in law
  - Debate issues of justice specifically considering their impact on liberty and equality
  - Reflect on impacts of legislation with regards to promoting, permitting, or prohibiting certain behaviors
  - Accurately represent alternative points of view on controversial political issues and debate the implications of policies related to them
- Rhetoric Stage
  - Develop and deliver eloquent speeches on controversial political issues
  - Create proposed legislation to deal with contemporary societal problems and debate them with others
  - Articulate philosophical underpinnings of American government (or your home country, if you are not in the USA)
  - Evaluate the effectiveness and constitutionality of specific historical and contemporary policies

Economics

Economics includes a consideration of decision-making (typically revolving around money-related decisions) at both the individual and societal level. Reasoning economically involves recognition that resources/goods/time/etc.

are scarce, that decisions have costs and benefits, and through systematically examining this subject, we can be both better at personal finance and better at civic engagement as virtually every political debate has, at its root, an economic discussion. A starter list outlining key aspects of an economics curriculum includes:

- Grammar Stage
  - Understand scarcity and its impact on decision-making
  - Compare and contrast costs/benefits of particular individual and societal actions
  - Describe goods and services, the costs of producing/providing them, and prices
  - Explain how financial institutions (banks) play a role in society
  - Recognize the benefits of competition for consumers
  - Explain the importance of saving and investing
- Logic Stage
  - Debate impacts of societal policies on individuals in light of justice, of liberty, and of equality
  - Debate ideas of free trade, globalization, competition, etc.
  - Analyze the role and impact of government incentives (or disincentives) on economic decisions (at micro and macro scales)
  - Evaluate the impact of innovation and entrepreneurship in market-based societies (could use historical or contemporary examples)
  - Evaluate individual choices related to saving, spending, and investing
- Rhetoric Stage
  - Create entrepreneurial proposals and implement them if possible
  - Understand economic indicators and analyze the current and future state of the economy in light of such indicators
  - Explain monetary and fiscal policies and evaluate their impacts on society (macro and micro)

Science

The development of an awareness of science in the major fields of earth science, biology, chemistry, physics, and astronomy. A quality education in these will expose students to leading theories to explain natural processes currently, an understanding of theoretical developments over time, and an awareness of how science proceeds. A basic outline for essentials of your science curriculum includes:

- Grammar Stage
  - Learn basic foundations about forces, life cycles, habitats, weather and climate, and how nature always changes
  - Learn basic foundations about energy, transfer and transformation, the structures and functions of living things, anatomy, processes that shape the earth (geology), and the use of natural resources
  - Learn basic foundations about matter, systems within earth and learn basic foundations of astronomy: The universe, galaxies, and more emphasis on our solar system,
  - Train students to look for patterns, cause and effect, stability and change, and for impacts through observation
  - Learn to engage in scientific inquiry by defining problems, asking questions, developing models, planning and carrying out investigations, analyzing and interpreting data, and constructing explanations (guided explorations)
- Logic Stage
  - Survey biology (biological building blocks – DNA, plants, invertebrates, vertebrates, anatomy), earth science (biomes, geographical features, plate tectonics), astronomy (space, how astronomer's study space), chemistry (periodic table, matter, solutions, chemical reactions, acids and bases), & physics (force, motion, energy, thermodynamics, sound, light)
  - Basic statistical applications in science – measurements, measurement error, etc.
  - Distinguish between scientific data and interpretations
  - Learn to engage in scientific inquiry by defining problems, asking questions, developing models, planning and carrying out investigations, analyzing and interpreting data, and constructing explanations (guided explorations)
- Rhetoric Stage
  - Deeper surveys into biology (cell structure function and reproduction, genetics, theory of evolution, ecology, eukaryotes, plant biology, human body systems), chemistry (atomic structure, electrons/protons/neutrons, bonding and reactions, water and equilibrium, organic chemistry), and physics (motion, electricity and magnetism, engineering, quantum and atomic physics)

- Distinguish among reasonable interpretations of the same data critically examining the explanatory power of competing theories
- Learn to engage in scientific inquiry by defining problems, asking questions, developing models, planning and carrying out investigations, analyzing and interpreting data, and constructing explanations (guided and independent explorations)

Mathematics

The study of mathematics is a crucial element of any person's learning for much of what we know about the world is based on measurement of the world (which requires math!). Mathematics is, quite literally, the language the universe is written in and our discovery of math has been one of the most important discoveries of all time. The cultivation of mathematical understanding is essential for a well-rounded student, especially in a world where people offer the lie that math is just a social construct. We need to equip our learners with a healthy understanding of mathematics and how its discovery has aided mankind in examining the world. A basic outline for essentials of your mathematics curriculum includes:

- Grammar Stage
  - Understand how mathematics helps us understand the world around us
  - Recognize numbers and perform basic arithmetic (addition, subtraction, rounding, estimation, measurement, shapes and patterns)
  - Memorize times tables
  - Perform computation for multiplication and division; learn fractions, decimals, percentages and their relationships)
  - Order of Operations
- Logic Stage
  - Understand how to utilize mathematics to measure unobservable entities and consider issues related to measurement, error, implications for conclusions drawn from it
  - Proportions, integer operations, solving equations, percentages, substitution
  - Basic Algebra (Graphing functions, creating expressions, linear functions, trend lines, scatterplots, irrational numbers, exponents, identify essential theorems) and Geometry (proportionality, volume and lateral surface area of shapes, sum of angles, etc.)

- Basic Statistics (Variables – IV/DV, Measures of Central Tendency and Variance, Probability, Data Displays)
- Rhetoric Stage
  - Understand how mathematics is used to predict unobservable entities
  - Algebra II and Trigonometry (functions, relations, linear equations, quadratic functions, complex numbers, exponential and logarithmic functions, trigonometric and circular functions, etc.)
  - Statistics (probability, variables, data analysis, statistical analyses)
  - Calculus (limits and continuity, derivatives and rates of change, integrals and area)

Reading

There are much more detailed accounts out there on the essentials of reading but I want to focus in on the key ideas that carry across the discipline. Throughout, there are several key foci: (1) Comprehension – knowledge of the text and the society in which it is written, (2) thematic analysis – examining authorial intent in light of contextual factors, (3) structural conventions – how the structure of text contributes to its meaning, and (4) language analysis – the details of a text's language contribute to its meaning. Above all, learners should be read to and be reading many, many books. In particular, the *great books* – those that transcend time and speak across ages and places. A basic outline for essentials of your reading curriculum includes:

- Grammar Stage
  - Have daily teacher-led read-alouds with high-quality books to expose children to eloquent use of language
  - Letter and sound recognition should be the primary learning aim early on
  - Including a small collection of high frequency words to know by seeing – "the"
  - Systematic phonics with explicit instruction (phonemic awareness, phonics, vocabulary, fluency, and reading comprehension)
  - Memorize poetry that is beautiful and interesting
  - Provide protected time daily for reading, much of it for individual choice reading but also for one-on-one reading where learners work on relevant readers with supervision

Table 8.1 A Small Collection of Recommended Great Books

Early Great Books	Middle Great Books	Later Great Books
Bible Stories	*The Hobbit & Lord of the Rings*, J.R.R. Tolkien	*1984*, George Orwell
Aesop's Fables	*Robinson Crusoe*, Daniel Defoe	*Last of the Mohicans*, J.F. Cooper
Fairy Tales, Hans Christian Anderson	*Treasure Island*, R.L. Stevenson	*Starship Troopers*, Robert Heinlein
Wind in the Willows, Keneth Grahame	*Island of the Blue Dolphins*, Scott O'Dell	*The Grapes of Wrath*, J. Steinbeck
Little House on the Prairie, Laura Ingalls Wilder	*Sherlock Holmes Series*, Arthur Conan Doyle	*The Talisman*, Sir Walter Scott
Peter Rabbit, Beatrix Potter	*The Story of King Arthur and His Knights*, Howard Pyle	*Hamlet, Merchant of Venice, Others*, William Shakespeare
The Iliad & Odyssey (adapted for kids)	*Huckleberry Finn & Tom Sawyer*, Mark Twain	*The Pilgrim's Progress*, John Bunyan
Classic Starts Books (B&N)	*My Side of the Mountain*, J.C. George	*Divine Comedy*, Dante Aligheri
Charlotte's Web, E.B. White	*Animal Farm*, George Orwell	*Canterbury Tales*, Geoffrey Chaucer
Chronicles of Narnia, C.S. Lewis	*The Lord of the Flies*, William Golding	*City of God*, Augustine
Swiss Family Robinson, Johann Wyss		*Crime and Punishment*, Feodor Dostoyevsky
		War and Peace, Leo Tolstoy
		The Great Gatsby, F.S. Fitzgerald

- o Learners should read more and more quality books as time continues, Table 8.1 above provides some recommended books, although it is by no means an all-inclusive list
- ◆ Logic Stage
  - o Instruction in critically examining high quality books – focus on mastering the elements of literature: theme, conflict, exposition, rising action, climax, falling action, and conclusion
    - o Identify these elements within the book you are reading
    - o Discuss to what extent you agree with the author's intentions
  - o Distinguish among common types of conflict within stories: Man versus God; man versus society; man versus nature; man versus man; man versus self

- Critically examine how books end: What does the resolution imply the author wants us to think about? How could he/she have done this differently? Why might they do this?
- Compare various types of literature including poetry, drama, prose, nonfiction, etc.
- Learners should continue reading high quality books, refer to Table 8.1 for examples
◆ Rhetoric Stage
  - Engage in purposeful Socratic Discussions with those who have collectively read the same book
  - Clarify the author's intended meaning and distinguish that from applications of that
  - Compare great books for similarity and difference in terms of how they represent elements of literature, common types of conflict, etc.
  - Learners should continue reading high quality books, refer to Table 8.1 for examples

Language Arts

Students need to have a strong grasp of the effective use of the written word. As such, strong understanding of grammar and punctuation are critical. Students should be trained to write clearly, coherently, and through use of language in support of their efforts to articulate their message for a range of contexts, purposes, and audiences. A basic outline for essentials of your language arts curriculum includes:

◆ Grammar Stage
  - Build vocabulary – leverage high quality read-alouds to expose learners to rich vocabulary
  - Grammar, punctuation, and composition
  - Learn about different purposes for and types of writing
  - Provide many models for imitation – a collection of exemplars – employ copy work from these so that early development includes copying from the highest quality work as their own
◆ Logic Stage
  - Build vocabulary – continue to introduce rich vocabulary beyond the reading level of learners to continually grow
  - Critically examine writing to analyze its type and effectiveness in that are (explanatory, argumentative, persuasive, narrative, poetry, etc.)

- Continue to provide many models for imitation – a collection of exemplars
- Require frequent use of metaphor, analogy, and poetry to extend learning deeper
- Students should write for various purposes and for various audiences – consider requiring them to submit something for publication
♦ Rhetoric Stage
- Challenge students to reconstitute high quality work for a different purpose
- Focus on precision within writing – demand tightness on the meaning of words and the flow within writing
- Require coherent and elegant written and oral work
- Have students prepare and present – in written and oral form – high quality speeches for various purposes

Foreign Languages

Students ought to be trained in a way that broadens their knowledge base and equips them to learn in domains beyond just English. Selection of specific languages is largely a contextual one – for those living along the southern border, Spanish makes great sense; however, in other areas, Mandarin may make more sense. Furthermore, classic languages, which have heavy influence on the English language provide leverage for our own language master. The educational leaders ought to reflect on the goals for their school and align the optional and/or required languages to make sense in light of those. A basic outline for essentials of your foreign language curriculum includes:

♦ Grammar Stage
- Learn the alphabet for the language and the sounds associated with letters
- Learn common rules and specific rules of the language
- Memorize simple statements in the language
- Speak conversationally using simple language
♦ Logic Stage
- Read simple works in the foreign language
- Practice translation of simple works
- Speak conversationally using the language at increasingly complex levels

- Practice translation for the purpose of word-for-word translation (Formal Equivalence) and for thought-for-thought translation (Functional Equivalence) discussing implications of each approach
- Rhetoric Stage
  - Compare translations with original text and critique them
  - Complete full translations of high-quality works from other languages
  - View videos or speeches in another foreign language to further immerse ability to hear the language as well as to see it
  - Deliver speeches in the foreign language

While I would recommend that each teacher and/or school consider the languages which seem to offer most contextual benefit, there are classical languages to consider as well. It seems impossible to deny the overwhelming benefits that studying Latin has for learners. Knowledge of the Latin language is not only beneficial in its help in learning other Latin-derived languages (Spanish, French, etc.) but more directly has immediate leverage to understanding in the sciences and other domains. For instance, one who learns Latin will learn the suffix of *ology*, which means study. When they encounter Biology, Geology, Anthropology, they are able to immediately use their Latin knowledge to anticipate what to encounter – Biology – the study of life; Geology – the study of earth; Anthropology – the study of man. Or another quick example: A student who learns Latin will understand the root word of *peri* means around. When he or she encounters the mathematics concept of perimeter, they will immediately have a leg up on remembering what it means because perimeter is the length *around* an object. All of these are important to have because they are able to bring up information into their mind related to these fields before diving in, which makes encoding of new information in their memory faster, easier, and more enduring. As such, it would be silly to not recognize Latin as crucial and, arguably, the single most important foreign language for those of us for whom English is the primary language we speak.

Technology

All too often, people's views about technology are polarized. On one side of the spectrum are the self-classified *21st century learning advocates* who see it as a must for everything. On the other end are those who view it as almost evil and consider reading on a device to be perhaps an outright sin and affront to *real* reading. Both of these ends are way off base. While I am an advocate for technology, I do want to offer a consistent message that we should explicitly instruct learners about certain important technologies but aside of that, we ought to be cautious about it. The integration of technology has been widely studied and interestingly, in many cases, it does not help, but rather hinders learning[1]. But we live in a society that is infused with technology and to refuse to leverage it when it can be appropriate in the learning environment is just as foolish an idea. A wise educator will reflect on what important aspects of technology can be leveraged for enhancing learning and lived experience and leave the rest out. A basic outline for essentials of your technology curriculum includes:

- Grammar Stage
  - Understand how to operate electronic devices, especially for data entry
  - Develop basic skills in typing on a computer (at least 25 WPM)
- Logic Stage
  - Develop skill to type on a computer efficiently (at least 50–60 WPM)
  - Understand how to use graphics and computer tools to enhance writing (smart art, images, tables, graphs, etc.)
  - Compare and contrast quality presentations using technology and *not* using technology
  - Critique news from various outlets examining their social media and full site displays
- Rhetoric Stage
  - Understand how to use technology to enhance presentation delivery (not flashy presentations but wisely developed ones that organize & enhance their oral delivery)
  - Create and submit a contribution to an online outlet (could be news, religious, educational, etc.)
  - Differentiate between uses of technology that enhance and distract from presentation quality

I would like to close with a few points to take away with regards to technology. First off, do not get too caught up in the current rush towards everything STEM (Science, Technology, Engineering, and Mathematics). While STEM is likely a key point to win a grant since it is prioritized based on societal trends, it is not the key to preparing students for success in life. Even Google learned its lesson when it completed a study of its hiring, firing, and promotion data to find out what qualities were most important for those who made a difference in the company. What they found was STEM expertise was actually ranked dead last in terms of those that predicted the paths of success[2]. Instead, the skills that emerged at the top are those that have typically been associated with a liberal education (which is, also commonly referred to as classical education) – communicating, listening, empathy towards other points of view, critical thinking, problem solving, seeing connections across complex ideas. So, be sure to include technology aspects into your education but do not do so to the devaluation of the other areas because technology is just a tool, without the knowledge from the other domains, we will be using that tool without the knowledge to use it well.

Secondly, and more importantly, we would be wise to ensure that our learners have much more time face-to-face with other individuals in authentic settings *without* technology being present than they do with it. As our society has seen technology become more and more pervasive, we are seeing several negative side effects that have been documented as highly linked to technology use (especially social media). This has resulted in two specific issues to be wary of: (1) Increasingly, we build our own insular echo chambers and (2) increasingly, we are losing our capacity for authentic relationships. For instance, Cass Sunstein (2017), in *#Republic* explains how social media has been a major force for decay in civil discourse because we use it to get filtered news and information that is always spun the way we want it. And if we don't like how it is presented, we *unfollow*. Similarly, Jean Twenge (2014) explains in *Generation Me* that in large part due to heavy use of technology, the generations of youth who grew up with technology since birth are more disengaged, narcissistic, distrustful, anxious, and entitled than other generations. Finally, and perhaps most important is a recently revised work from Sherry Turkle (2017), *Alone Together*. Turkle has studied technology and its impact on human behavior and relationships for several decades. She began very optimistic about its potential but that optimism has largely ceded to pessimism about its negative impacts on us. Surrounding ourselves with technology leaves us constantly distracted, losing our capacity for solitude; we settle for less empathy, less attention, and less care from other human beings; we are more distracted in each other's company, and we know it; and Turkle explains that it is almost as if each of us "is tethered to a mobile device and to the people and places to which that device serves as a portal" (p. 155) rather than being present with one another. And when we give into the temptation to look at our device again, it is like giving in to a blackmailer; we think it makes us free but it only enslaves us further. We imagine technology to be an elixir of efficiency and possibility but largely it leads to disappointment, disengagement, and disenchantment, and even delusion.

These ramifications are significant and thus, we ought to significantly limit our use of technology *inside and outside* of the classroom. So, do not rule technology out simply because it is technology and "new" but instead, choose carefully considered times and contexts to leverage it to enhance learning or teach necessary skills and take caution to not let it take hold of our children.

Philosophy

One of the least common subject areas to find explicitly in our current educational system is that of philosophy. However, philosophy is essential as it underpins just about every other domain. While philosophy is commonly considered the love of wisdom, what it really boils down to is a focus on effective reasoning. Wisdom does not come from sheer experience; wisdom does not come from happenstance; wisdom emerges when one has sufficient knowledge, robust analytical skill, and is able to derive warranted conclusions. Philosophy is a gateway to wisdom but the wise person is really he or she who is capable of seeing things in the big picture. This requires a breadth and depth of knowledge and a humility, which only comes through a rich knowledge-base, wide experience, and awareness of good or poor reasoning. Philosophy helps us in this last necessary aspect of developing wisdom – being aware of higher and lower quality reasoning in any domain. It is foolish for someone to say: "I don't care about philosophy". Everyone is a philosopher. The question is not: Are you a philosopher? The question is rather: Are you a good philosopher or a bad philosopher?

Philosophy in a simple sense is essential in that it governs our interactions with ideas. And ideas have consequences. Ideas govern both our own personal decision-making as well as systemic affairs in human societies. Awareness of one's own presuppositions – an essential element of philosophy – is necessary for moving from knowledgeable to wise. In fact, any attempt to draw an inference from information requires philosophical competence – or if philosophical ignorance exists, those inferences are often silly, distracting, erroneous, and ultimately unhelpful to the advance of knowledge. It is in this way that philosophy allows for tighter precision in all the domains.

Some very big-named scientists have shunned philosophy only to be noted for their ignorance by those with a sharper awareness of philosophy. For instance, Neil DeGrasse-Tyson and Michio Kaku[3], both attempt to use their knowledge of theoretical physics or astronomy as a means to draw inferences about the supernatural – in this instance, claiming that science has proven that there is nothing non-material[4]. In effect, this is what some researchers refer to as *epistemic trespassing*, when someone judges matters outside their field of expertise (Ballantyne, 2018). And unfortunately, their lack of philosophical awareness leaves them susceptible to such ignorance – even amongst some of the most intellectual giants of our contemporary age. Their scientific findings do not speak about philosophical and metaphysical issues; rather they presuppose views about them and when they speak on philosophy, they are outside of their realm of expertise. So, yes. Philosophy matters. It matters a great deal, actually. So, what sorts of essentials would be included in a philosophy domain for our learners in this 21st Century Trivium?

Below is a list of organized topics and ideas to include for philosophy in the 21st century trivium:

- Grammar Stage
  - Lay foundations for clear thinking on issues
    - Agreeing on a definition before debating/critiquing/applying
    - Ensuring accuracy of views as paramount
    - Distinguishing between fact, opinion, inference, etc. (in real-world situations and in dealing with primary/secondary sources, e.g.)
    - Clarifying premises and conclusions within informal and formal arguments
    - Establish existence of laws of logic: law of identity; law of non-contradiction
  - Train in effective observation skills that are objective
- Logic Stage
  - Formal Logic Introduction
  - Explicit instruction on logical Fallacies
  - Debates on Philosophical Issues emphasizing defining terms and clarifying the essence of a thing (e.g., Is it possible to find truth in history? Does CO2 cause global warming?)
  - Emphasize the importance of knowing why you believe what you believe
  - Anticipate counterpoints to arguments
  - Build argument comparison charts and evaluate evidence types/quality (corroborating, circumstantial, possible/probable, possible biases, how feelings skew)
  - Describe good scientific inquiry
- Rhetoric Stage
  - Formal Logic Advanced
  - Illustrate good scientific inquiry and discuss/explore how to use it while critiquing poor applications of it

- Debates on Philosophical Issues (e.g., Is the mind independent of the brain? Does God exist? Is time travel possible?)
- Evaluations of Political Issues (e.g., Abortion, Originalism, Capital Punishment, Flat versus Progressive Tax Rates)

Before wrapping up this section on philosophy, it is essential to note that typically a thorough education must include the subject of *theology*. The questions of human nature, existence, origins, meaning, destiny, and so forth are arguably the most important issues to explore. However, thanks to various court rulings in public school settings, this is not currently an easy route to navigate. So, I want to note that, first and foremost, I disagree with the notion that theological learning is not part of a rounded education – exploring the matters of life beyond this life is an essential aspect of developing a human fully. But, since it is unfortunately the case that religion is largely left out of schools, I want to wrap up and bring this into the discussion in two very brief ways. First off, for those in a position to integrate theology into your instruction, I cannot encourage it enough. If this is the case, I will point readers to a few other sources that are worth exploring for those interested in what this might look like in the footnotes[5]. Secondly, if you are not able to bring theology directly into your curriculum, you can integrate religion more generally into your philosophy program. After all, a theology is a philosophical presupposition – you could argue that it is *the* ontological (basis from which all else flows) philosophy.

In any account, learning about religions in an appropriate manner should not focus on their superficial similarities but rather their fundamental distinctions. Consider helping students understand these fundamental differences because this is where knowledge is of more consequence for individual and societal affairs. These are the areas where theological study matters – it is not in the practices of religion that we find relevant material to learn, it is in the beliefs surrounding the ultimate questions that have mankind has pondered for millennia – how did we get here? Where are we going? Why does this world have such difficulty? What ultimate meaning is there in life? It should go without saying that in the public education environment, the teacher should not engage of any type of evangelism nor preaching any particular dogma including secular religions such as Wokism[6]. So, consider integrating theology into your curriculum directly as a standalone subject matter or indirectly, by including examination of the theological answers of religions to these ultimate questions in your philosophy program so that students get the opportunity in their formal learning experience to engage with the ultimate questions of life.

Summary

This chapter surveyed a good number of broad disciplines of learning that educators should be aware of. This should provide readers with a general sense of essential content and important skills to consider in each of those domains as well as generate ideas for overlap across classes where possible. This is not considered an exhaustive list of all relevant topics, but it is intended to hit on those that are most prominent and of significance.

For Reflection and Application

Thinking back on this chapter, consider the following reflective tasks and ideas for application in your classroom:

1 Look specifically at one of the domains presented in this chapter that is most related to what you do and review the recommended elements to consider at each of these stages.
    a. Reflect on the extent to which your course does this and consider ways you can place increased emphasis on them, if appropriate.
    b. Reflect on important topics in what you teach and how these essentials relate to those. Can you meaningfully connect them?
2 Look specifically at several of the domains presented in this chapter that you typically spend less time on. Are there aspects from those that you can connect to help learners see connections that they might not see on their own?
3 Consider working with colleagues – or by yourself – to try and look across all these domains or subject matters? Although research does not currently support the notion of transferrable skills, considering domain-specific skills that link with others could provide a healthy consideration of uniting aspects of our teaching in different domains. Try to identify some of them and consider how you might leverage them.

Notes

1. Wood, E., Zivcakova, L., Gentile, P., Archer, K., De Pasquale, D., & Nosko, A. (2012). Examining the impact of off-task multitasking with technology on real-time classroom learning. *Computers & Education*, 58, 365–374.

2. Here is a 2017 article from the Washington Post that reflects on the fact that it was classical liberal arts skills and not STEM training that was what even tech companies wanted: https://www.washingtonpost.com/news/answer-sheet/wp/2017/12/20/the-surprising-thing-google-learned-about-its-employees-and-what-it-means-for-todays-students/?noredirect=on&utm_term=.91aa77a655d9
3. I must admit these are two of my favorites, too, in that their ability to make science interesting for lay people is wonderful. I own four of Kaku's book's in particular ☺. However, as I note here, both tend to wade into philosophical speculation without seemingly being aware that they are moving beyond their domain of competence and thus showcase a hubris that detracts from their generally great work. A person with even a basic philosophical training could spot when they are moving beyond the bounds of what they are warranted in saying.
4. I should also note that Dr. Kaku actually seems to have backed off of some earlier anti-theistic views and has adopted a view that 'God' exists and he imagines him as some form of cosmic music. In any account, these are philosophical speculations by a physicist who is not primarily a philosopher.
5. Readers should check out Douglas Wilson (1991) *Recovering the lost tools of learning*, in particular Appendix B provides some specific suggestions on this; another good resource is Robert Littlejohn & Charles T. Evans (2006), *Wisdom and Eloquence,* which throughout build a powerful case for philosophy and theology as the "true sciences".
6. The religious nature of applied postmodernism has been noted widely – here is a link to an electronic source articulating this well: https://areomagazine.com/2018/12/18/postmodern-religion-and-the-faith-of-social-justice/ and another calling it one of America's new religions: https://nymag.com/intelligencer/2018/12/andrew-sullivan-americas-new-religions.html?utm_source=tw.

9

Conclusion

We must strive to be worthy of an inheritance that we did not, ourselves, create. And when we feel the urge to change that inheritance, we ought to be prudent to be sure that we first truly understand it. Piety is not something that should be bound exclusively to the altar and to religion; rather, it ought to be an attitude for life[1]. So, we should have no desire to escape from the past. Instead, we ought to study it and to look for those timeless ideas that keep holding on – they are, for us, the distilled wisdom of the ages. From this distilled wisdom, we are able to fulfill our obligation to the present by our requisite engagement with the past for the obligation of ensuring wisdom is passed on to impact the future.

By committing to utilize this framework, you enter into a great, classical, and evidence-informed tradition. You are a part of an enduring community of those who desire learning for its own sake and who will not let sacred cows, pet philosophies, or even those favorite activities distract us from constant pursuit of learning. One of the single best things that we might do for our students is to change where they are looking. Largely because of our current emphasis on student-centered education, we ask students to use a mirror on everything. What does this mean to you? How does this connect to you? Why is this relevant for you? Do the next generation a favor and toss the mirror away and point them to a window. Let's not continue to perpetuate the idea that everything is about them; rather, let's help them look out and look at everything else.

Four Necessary Commitments

So, to close out, let us consider some things we ought to commit to as we move forward in building better learning environments. The very first thing is to ensure that we affirm that the work we are doing to help equip others to learn is incredibly important.

Commitment #1: Know That What You Are Doing Matters

During your time leading instruction, there is nothing more important than what you are doing. This is your pulpit and you have something that is very important to convey. Do not forget that. As engineer of the learning experience for your learners, you cannot permit frivolous activities or a haphazard meandering of the class. Every moment counts. We need to know the specific purpose for our lesson and our designed learning experience must move us towards that aim by design; we cannot leave that to chance. Additionally, we must stay focused on that purpose.

Furthermore, because what we are doing is so important, we cannot simply "cover" the information, we must take deliberate action to check for understanding prior to, during, after, and beyond so as to continually, and effectively, adapt our instruction. We establish and commit to procedures that prioritize learning, not preference. Key questions are prepared in advance so that we can guarantee that they are introduced, examined, and addressed sufficiently. Finally, as the teacher and leader in the classroom, model a reverence for the subject and express your interest in excellence in it. Take the time to know your stuff so that you can translate it to the learners' levels. Be passionate. Adapt your instruction to the background knowledge and experience your learners have (not their preferences, their knowledge/experience). There simply is nothing more important than equipping your students for their lives; never forget that.

Commitment #2: Know Why What You Are Doing Matters

If you adopt this framework, then you are committing to an education that equips learners with tools of learning so that you empower them to become self-learners. We must acknowledge our ultimate aims for education lest we allow weaker, shallow, and ephemeral reasons to take our students' minds. Education is not about getting you a job; it is not about getting you into college – those are doors that will open up with a meaningful education but they are not the ends. The real aims of education include the pursuit of truth, the cultivation of goodness, the appreciation of beauty, and preparing one to examine what it means to be human. These are the ultimate aims and they, unlike much of what we hear today, do not fade away. As a teacher, you must model the virtues of learning because of this importance: Wonder at the beauty, majesty, and mystery of the world; display your curiosity; demand precision – of your students and yourself; be elegant in your speech; model order and a commitment to excellence. And because you know why this is so important you must also convey it to your learners. Unveil the playbook for their path and invite them to join you on this quest to examine what it means to be human and how best to pursue happiness.

Taking on this mission will ensure that you give your learners the best experience that they can have so that they are a truly educated individual who is knowledgeable, who is wise beyond his or her years, and who is ready to put his or her skills to anything that he or she encounters. And they are equipped with tools to succeed.

Commitment #3: Know the Essential Principles of Learning and Apply Them in Your Classroom

Try a little recall exercise to help strengthen your memory of these principles by first jotting down the principles as you remember them. Then, skip back to Chapters One and Two to revisit them again in a more in-depth look if necessary or continue on as we will explore some instructional implications of each of these for your classroom in the next section.

While we must acknowledge that it is true that every learner is unique and his or her prior knowledge is crucial in building bridges to richer understanding, these principles hold true for learning in all contexts. So, we can both adapt for our individual's context but also hold firm to those principles, which transcend them providing a healthy balance of science of learning to inform the art of instruction.

Commitment #4: Know How to Leverage the Trivium to Build Environments That Cultivate Learning

Recall that insofar as we are using the trivium for guidance in instruction in the framework, envisioning them as stages is appropriate and helpful. First, we must build up essential knowledge in the topic that we are exploring ensuring that we have accurate understanding of foundations. This is our grammar stage. Next, we exercise our reasoning skills as we introduce nuance, engage with the complexity of concepts and ideas, looking for rules and patterns that underlie a domain while enhancing understanding and demanding precision in our words. It dives deeply into broadly touched topics in the grammar stage and simultaneously may introduce new information to increase the broad base of knowledge that we have as well. This is our logic stage. Third, we challenge learners to articulate their understanding through elegant expression. Furthermore, we convey the importance of taking time to draw conclusions, to derive inferences, and to seek and persuade others. In this way our learner's capstone experience intentionally builds wisdom and challenges them to be eloquent and engaged individuals. This is our rhetoric stage.

Through this process, if our students encounter it again and again, they will become empowered for self-learning because you took time to build an effective learning environment. This pattern becomes their pattern and your learners will learn how to take responsibility for their own learning when it falls on them to do so. They will propose solutions rather than just offer up complaints. They will be grateful in spite of the struggles as they aim towards the truest ends of learning. And you will have empowered them to do so because you took the time to engage with the best current evidence and the wisdom of the past to build an effective learning environment.

For Reflection and Application

1. Complete a one-page summary of this book to share highlights with your colleagues.
2. Revisit your curriculum in light of the 21st Century Trivium Framework and adapt it.
3. Reflect on the four commitments herein and decide what to do now.

Note

1. I have adapted this form the late Roger Scruton who offered similar comments.

Appendix A: The Dime

Pictures of the Dime

By United States Mint - http://www.usmint.gov/pressroom/index.cfm?flash=no&action=photo#Pres, Public Domain, https://commons.wikimedia.org/w/index.php?curid=31105184

'Heads' Side of the Dime

The head displayed on the dime (current as of June 2018) is of President Franklin D. Roosevelt.

'Tails' Side of the Dime

The tails displayed a torch in the middle, an olive branch to the left, and an oak branch to the right. The torch is understood to stand for liberty. The oak branch stands for victory. And the olive branch represents being willing to extend an olive branch, if appropriate.

The Three Phrases on Every Single American Coin (since 1956)

1. Liberty
2. In God We Trust
3. E Pluribus Unum

Appendix B: Dr. K's Checklist for Evaluating Scientific Claims on Learning

Instructions to Use

This handout walks through the *S.E.A.R.CH process* for how to interact with new scientific evidence. It includes only the aspects that can be clearly translated into marking as positive or negative.

- If, overall, most of the items you mark fall into the plus category, I think you have good reason to put the study and its claims into the consider pile.
- If, however, most fall in the minus, I would not consider its findings.
- If results are quite mixed, I would put it in a folder for looking at later as more studies are found that look at the topic

A final caveat: recall that one study is almost never sufficient to make any significant changes. We are interested in the pursuit of truth, which given our finitude should focus on the preponderance of evidence.

STEP 1: S (*Simply state the claim*)	YES (+)	NO (−)	COMMENTS/ NOTES
• Have I eliminated all emotional appeals from the claim? • Have I considered both the claim and its opposite – or alternatives? • Have I identified and removed as evidence any feelings of familiarity with this idea? • Have I identified and removed as evidence any feelings of popularity with this idea? • Have I identified and removed as evidence any positive feelings associated with the person affiliated with this idea?			
STEP 2: E (*Examine the authority*)			
• Does the authority have a terminal degree in the specific area they are speaking on? • Does the authority have peer reviewed publications on the topic at hand? • Does the authority have other publications on the topic at hand? • Is the authority recognized as an expert on the topic at hand? • Is the authority the original creator of the idea? • Is empirical evidence shared to support the claim?			

STEP 3: A (*Assess the quality of evidence*)			
• Does the evidence show that this improves learning directly? • Where does the evidence fit in terms of the Quality of Evidence hierarchy? (Figure 5.2) • Do the researchers share their assumptions? And do you find them reasonable? • Is the sample representative (reflect the people it is supposed to be true of?) • Is there a high proportion of both participation and completion in the study? • Are groups compared in the study? • Do groups have equal treatment aside from one variable? • Is the work free from bias? • Are the measures valid/reliable? • Do the measures focus on objective data? • Is it clear that no results have been omitted or framed to only focus on one view? • Do the claims make sense in light of the evidence or are they unwarranted?			
STEP 4: R (*Reflect on conflicting data*)			
• Is any possible conflicting evidence shared? • Do your ratings find the claim generally supported?			
STEP 5: CH (*Choose if it should influence you*)			
• Based on your overall SEARCHing of this topic, do you believe it is worth changing your approach to teaching/learning now?			

Next Steps

What specifically should you do? (If you do not know anything specific to do, then honestly it doesn't matter at this point except perhaps to continue reading – science does not always neatly translate to application, if so, wait and see).

How will you know if it is working? When will you confirm this? (Write these down, measure the impacts, and if it is not translating to positive impact consider stopping it and waiting/looking for more information)

Appendix C: Dr. K's What's in the Ballpark Activity (Blank Copy)

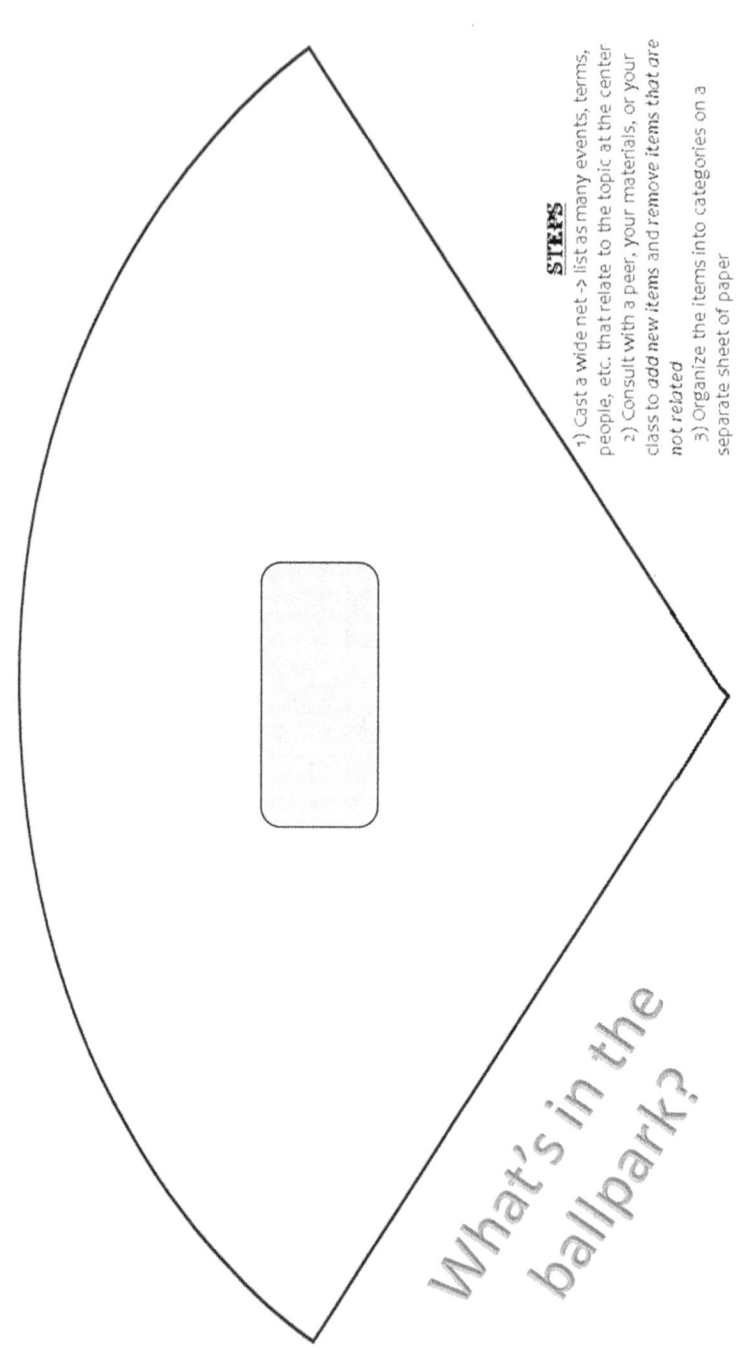

References

Atkinson, R.K., Derry, S.J., Renkl, A., & Wortham, D. (2000). Learning from examples: Instructional principles from worked examples research. *Review of educational research*, 70(2): 181–214.

Avicenna, *Metaphysics* 1; commenting on Aristotle, Topics I.1.105a4-5.

Ballantyne, N. (2018). Epistemic trespassing. *Mind* (forthcoming at time of publication).

Bower, G.H. (1978). Experiments on story comprehension and recall. *Discourse processes*, 1: 211–231.

Chen, O., Kalyuga, S., & Sweller, J. (2016). When instructional guidance is needed. *Educational and Developmental Psychologist*, 33: 149–162.

Clark, R.E. (1982). Antagonism between achievement and enjoyment in ATI studies. *Educational psychologist*, 17(2): 92–101.

Clark, R.C., & Mayer, R.E. (2003). *E-learning and the science of instruction: Proven guidelines for consumers and designers of multimedia learning*. San Francisco, CA: Jossey-Bass.

Clark, R.C., & Mayer, R.E. (2016). *E-learning and the science of instruction: Proven guidelines for consumers and designers of multimedia learning*. Hoboken, NJ: John Wiley & Sons.

Cowan, N. (2010). The magical mystery four: How is working memory capacity limited, and why? *Current Direct Psychological Science*, 19(1): 51–57. Available online: <https://www.ncbi.nlm.nih.gov/pmc/articles/PMC2864034/>.

Dale, E. (1946). *Audio-visual methods in teaching*. New York, NY: Dryden Press, 1954, 1969.

Egan, K. (2005). *An imaginative approach to teaching*. San Francisco, CA: Jossey-Bass.

Eliot, T.S. (1951). Religion and literature essay, in *Selected essays: 1917-1932*, revised edition. San Diego, CA: Harcourt.

Ericsson, K.A. (2016). *Peak: Secrets from the new science of expertise*. New York, NY: Houghton-Mifflin Harcourt.

Feynman, R. (1985). *Surely, you're joking Mr. Feynman!* New York, NY: W.W. Norton & Company.

Freire, P. (2000). *Pedagogy of the oppressed*. Translated by Myra Bergman Ramos. New York, NY: Continuum.

Garon-Carrier, G., Boivin, M., Guay, F., Kovas, Y., Dionne, G., Lemelin, J. … Tremblay, R.E. (2016). Intrinsic motivation and achievement in mathematics in elementary school: A longitudinal investigation of their association. *Child development*, 87(1): 165–175.

Gladwell, M. (2008). *Outliers: The story of success*. New York, NY: Little: Brown and Company.

Glenn, C.L. (2003). Fanatical secularism. *Education next*, Winter: 60–65.

Graesser, A.C., Singer, M., & Trabasso, T. (1994). Constructing inferences during narrative text comprehension. *Psychological review*, 101: 371–395.

Hannust, T., & Kikas, E. (2007). *Children's knowledge of astronomy and its change in the course of learning. Early Childhood Research Quarterly*, 22(1): 89–104.

Hattie, J. (2009). *Visible learning: A synthesis of over 800 meta-analyses relating to achievement*. New York, NY: Routledge.

Hirsch, E.D. (1988). *Cultural literacy: What every American needs to know*. New York, NY: Vintage Books.

Jones, C., & Shao, B. (2011). *The net generation and digital natives: Implications for higher education*. York, UK: Higher Education Academy.

Kalyuga, S., Ayres, P., Chandler, P., & Sweller, J. (2003). The expertise reversal effect. *Educational Psychologist*, 38(1): 23–31.

Kennedy, D.M., & Fox, B. (2013). "Digital natives": An Asian perspective for using learning technologies. *International journal of education & development using information & communication technology*, 9(1): 64–79.

Kirschner, P.A., & van Merrienboer, J.J.G. (2013). Do learners really know best? Urban legends in education. *Educational Psychology*, 48(3): 1–15.

Krahenbuhl, K.S. (2016). Student-centered education and constructivism: Challenges, concerns, and clarity for teachers. *The clearing house: A journal of educational strategies, issues, and ideas*, 89(3): 97–105.

Krahenbuhl, K.S. (2018). *The decay of truth in education: Implications and ideas for its restoration*. Newcastle upon Tyne, UK: Cambridge Scholars.

Lalley, J.P., & Miller, R.H. (2007). The learning pyramid: Does it point teachers in the right direction? *Education*, 128(1): 64–80.

Mayer, R.E. (2001). *Multimedia learning*. New York, NY: Cambridge University Press.

Mayer, R.E. (2004). Should there be a three-strikes rule against pure discovery learning? The case for fully guided methods of instruction. *American Psychologist*, 59(1): 1–14.

Miller, G.A. (1956). The magical number seven, plus or minus two: Some limits on our capacity for processing information. *Psychological Review*, 101(2): 343–352. Available online: <http://psych.utoronto.ca/users/peterson/psy430s2001/Miller%20GA%20Magical%20Seven%20Psych%20Review%201955.pdf.

Mousavi, S.Y., Low, R., & Sweller, J. (1995). Reducing cognitive load by mixing auditory and visual presentation modes. *Journal of Educational Psychology*, 87: 319–334.

Pashler, H., Bain, P.M., Bottge, B.A., Graesser, A., Koedinger, K., McDaniel, M., & Metcalfe, J. (2007). *Organizing instruction and study to improve student learning: IES practice Guide*. Washington, DC: National Center for Education Research, Institute of Education Sciences, U.S. Department of Education. Retrieved from http://ncer.ed.gov.

Pashler, H., McDaniel, M., Rohrer, D., & Bjork, R. (2009). Learning styles: Concepts and evidence. *Psychological science in the public interest*, 9(3): 105–119.

Pieper, J. (2009). *Leisure: The basis of culture, with forward from James Schall*. San Francisco, CA: Ignatius Press.

Postman, N. (2005). *Amusing ourselves to death: Public discourse in the age of show business*. New York, NY: Penguin.

Rohrer, D., & Pashler, H. (2012). Learning styles: Where's the evidence? *Medical education*, 46: 630–635.

Sayers, D. (1948). *The lost tools of learning*. Text of speech available online at: http://triviumeducation.com/texts/The_Lost_Tools_of_Learning.pdf.

Sara, S.J. (2000). Retrieval and reconsolidation: Toward a neurobiology of remembering. *Learning & Memory*, 7: 73–84.

Schwartz, D.L., Tsang, J.M., & Blair, K.P. (2016). *The ABCs of how we learn: 26 scientifically proven approaches, how they work, and when to use them*. New York: NY.

Smith, M.A., Roediger, H.L., & Karpicke, I.I.I., J.D. (2013). Covert retrieval practice benefits retention as much as overt retrieval practice. *Journal of Experimental Psychology: Learning, memory and Cognition*, 39: 1712–1725.

Sunstein, C. (2017). *#Republic: Divided democracy in the age of social media*. Princeton, NJ: Princeton University Press.

Thorne, A. (2010). Beating the apple tree: How the university coerces activism. *Academic questions*, 23(2): 212–224.

Tulgan, B. (1999). *FAST feedback*. Amhert, MA: HRD Press, Inc.

Turkle, S. (2017). *Alone together: Why we expect more from technology and less form each other*. 3rd Ed. New York, NY: Basic Books.

Twenge, J. (2014). *Generation Me: Why Today's Young Americans are more confident, Assertive, entitled – And more miserable than ever Before*. New York, NY: Atria Paperback Books.

Willingham, D.T. (2004). Ask the cognitive scientist: The privileged status of story. *American educator*, 28(2): 43–45.

Wolf, M. (2018). *Reader come home: The reading brain in a digital world*. New York, NY: Harper Collins.

For Product Safety Concerns and Information please contact our EU representative GPSR@taylorandfrancis.com
Taylor & Francis Verlag GmbH, Kaufingerstraße 24, 80331 München, Germany

www.ingramcontent.com/pod-product-compliance
Lightning Source LLC
Chambersburg PA
CBHW080938300426
44115CB00017B/2868